Migration and Health: what we know so far, what is lacking in our understanding and how to move forward?

Migration and Health

WHAT WE KNOW SO FAR, WHAT IS LACKING IN OUR UNDERSTANDING AND HOW TO MOVE FORWARD?

2018

EDITORS
Sónia Dias, Jorge Simões, Pedro Pita Barros

ALMEDINA

MIGRATION AND HEALTH

EDITORS
Sónia Dias, Jorge Simões, Pedro Pita Barros

EDITOR
EDIÇÕES ALMEDINA, S.A.
Rua Fernandes Tomás, nºs 76, 78 e 79
3000-167 Coimbra
Tel.: 239 851 904 · Fax: 239 851 901
www.almedina.net · editora@almedina.net

DESIGN DE CAPA
FBA

PAGINAÇÃO
João Félix – Artes Gráficas

IMPRESSÃO E ACABAMENTO
Vasp - DPS

Junho, 2018
DEPÓSITO LEGAL
442290/18

ALMEDINA | GRUPOALMEDINA

BIBLIOTECA NACIONAL DE PORTUGAL – CATALOGAÇÃO NA PUBLICAÇÃO
MIGRATION AND HEALTH

Migration and health : what we know so far, what is lacking in our understanding and how to move forward? / coord. Sónia Dias, Jorge Simões, Pedro Pita Barros. – (Olhares sobre a saúde)
ISBN 978-972-40-7487-0

I – DIAS, Sónia
II – SIMÕES, Jorge
III – BARROS, Pedro Pita, 1966-

CDU 614

ACKNOWLEDGEMENTS

The Editors are grateful to the authors for their contribution to the book, as well as to all speakers and attendants who participated in the International Seminar "Migration and Health: what we know so far, what is lacking in our understanding and how to move forward?". Special thanks to Fundação Calouste Gulbenkian and Professor Jorge Soares for the partnership regarding the topic of migration and health. We thank Ana Gama and Onome Akpogheneta for their collaboration in revising the book.

INDEX

AUTHORS (ALPHABETIC ORDER)

Allan Krasnik, EUPHA, University of Copenhagen, European Public Health Association
Ana Gama, Global Health and Tropical Medicine, Instituto de Higiene e Medicina Tropical, Universidade NOVA de Lisboa
Antonio Chiarenza, AUSL-IRCCS of Reggio Emilia, Chair of the Task Force Migration, Equity and Diversity
Bernadette N. Kumar, Norwegian Centre for Minority Health Research (NAKMI)
Bernd Rechel, European Observatory on Health Systems and Policies
Camilla Michaëlis, University of Copenhagen
Cristina Casas, High Commission for Migration
David Ingleby, University of Amsterdam
Elena Val, International Organization of Migration
Federica Viello, International Organization of Migration
Inês Fronteira, Global Health and Tropical Medicine, Instituto de Higiene e Medicina Tropical, Universidade NOVA de Lisboa
Isabelle Beauclercq, International Organization of Migration
Jorge Simões, Global Health and Tropical Medicine, Instituto de Higiene e Medicina Tropical, Universidade NOVA de Lisboa
Luis Roxo, Global Health and Tropical Medicine, Instituto de Higiene e Medicina Tropical, Universidade NOVA de Lisboa
Teresa Tito de Morais, President of Portuguese Refugee Council
Palmira Immordino, World Health Organisation, Regional Office for Europe
Pedro Calado, High Commissioner of Migration
Roumyana Petrova-Benedict, International Organization of Migration

Santino Severoni, World Health Organisation, Regional Office for Europe
Sónia Dias, Global Health and Tropical Medicine, Instituto de Higiene e Medicina Tropical, Universidade NOVA de Lisboa.

FOREWORD

By Jorge Sampaio *

This collection of papers on the topical issue of migration and health is a very useful tool for all those who work in this field or just want to know more about it. As the triple question of the title shows – *Migration and Health: What we know so far, what is lacking in our understanding and how to move forward?* – this publication is underpinned by the need to map out the sector in order to identify the existing shortcomings and flaws and, on an evidence-based approach, define better health policies.

It is well known that governments are faced with the challenge of integrating the health needs of migrants into national plans and strategies as outlined since 2008 in the 61st World Health Assembly Resolution on Health of Migrants and reiterated in the 70th World Health Assembly Resolution on Promoting the Health of Refugees and Migrants, endorsed in May 2018.

This Resolution urges Member States to: 1) consider promoting the framework of priorities and guiding principles as appropriate at global, regional and country levels including using it to inform discussions among Member States and partners engaged in the development of the global

* President of the Portuguese Republic (1996-2006), UN Special Envoy to Stop Tuberculosis (2006-2012), Chairman of the Global Platform For Syrian Students

compact on refugees and the global compact for safe, orderly and regular migration; 2) identify and collect evidence-based information, best practices and lessons learned in addressing the health needs of refugees and migrants in order to contribute to the development of a draft global action plan on promoting the health of refugees and migrants; 3) strengthen international cooperation on the health of refugees and migrants in line with paragraphs 11 and 68 and other relevant paragraphs of the New York Declaration for Refugees and Migrants; 4) consider providing necessary health-related assistance through bilateral and international cooperation to those countries hosting and receiving large populations of refugees and migrants.

Against this backdrop, this Report is very timely and the studies it comprises are an important input to understand the challenges that exist not only in generating evidence but also in designing good public policies aimed at improving the integration of migrants into societies that are shaped by cohesion, equity and inclusiveness and that seek to ensure the provision of quality healthcare services for all.

The variety of cases across European countries as well as the legal, linguistic and cultural diversity covered by the various authors and the range of topics raised make of this book a very enriching and useful read that opens up new avenues for an informed discussion and helps navigate many complex issues and decision-making problems.

Lisbon, May 2018

INTRODUCTION

In the last decades, European countries have experienced an increase in immigration, making migration more common than ever and societies more diverse. Europe has constituted a destiny region for a growing number of migrants from diverse regions and cultures seeking economic and work opportunities, pursuing family reunion, fleeing from war contexts, among other reasons. During the migration process, migrant populations often have to adapt to new societal, cultural and linguistic contexts in the host countries. The current complexity of the migration phenomenon results in a heterogeneous migrant population with different characteristics and health needs across European countries.

In an increasingly globalized world, human mobility and migratory fluxes pose significant public health challenges in planning and implementing effective health policies and responsive health systems. These aspects must be considered in societies pursue for migrants' integration and for healthcare quality and equity in order to attain the wellbeing of the whole population. Indeed, migrant populations can contribute for the host countries by stimulating economic growth and demographic renewal. Also, it is broadly acknowledged that migrant health is key for a successful migrant integration process in host societies and therefore it is crucial that migrants are and remain healthy.

Research on the health impacts of migration has significantly increased over the years. It has giving a valuable contribution in pointing out evidence-based efforts and strategies that may effectively improve health gain among these populations. Yet, further efforts are still needed to help societies to become more inclusive and potentiate the benefits of a successful migrant integration.

This context inspired the NOVA Health – Universidade NOVA de Lisboa and the Institute of Hygiene and Tropical Medicine of Universidade Nova de Lisboa, in partnership with Calouste Gulbenkian Foundation, to organize the *International Seminar "Migration and Health: what we know so far, what is lacking in our understanding and how to move forward?"*, held in Lisbon in June 8th, 2017. The discussion of health issues associated with migration is more fruitful in an international context of experience and information sharing. Universidade Nova de Lisboa has a strong core of its activities in health-related aspects, ranging from basic research to health policies and patient bedside clinical decisions, with contribution of several disciplinary fields (medicine, public health, sociology, economics, etc.). Thus, Universidade Nova de Lisboa takes up in a natural way the challenge to lead the discussion of migrants and resulting health challenges.

The Seminar provided a view on what we know so far, what is lacking in our understanding and how to collectively move forward in order to achieve the ultimate goal of improving the health and wellbeing of migrant populations and societies in general. This Seminar provided an opportunity for debating these current hot topics at policy, research and intervention levels, gathering a wide audience of international and national stakeholders and experts in migration and health issues. Topics under debate included innovative ways of researching and intervening to act more efficiently and have greater impact in obtaining health gain. The book offers an informative overview of the compilation of contributions of invited speakers and aims to provide a comprehensive review of the state-of-art on migration and health issues and recommendations for sound research, policy development and future actions. It lays down themes and open questions for future research. The ten chapters of the book are quite comprehensive in the topics they cover.

The first chapter opens with a description of human mobility and global migration. It highlights the European public health challenges in hosting heterogeneous groups of migrants. The chapter offers an overview of the European migrant health policies, referring long term policies from both health and non-health sectors. In this sense, the authors highlight that it is imperative to promote an inter-sectoral approach in dealing with the multifaceted dynamic of migration. The chapter concludes by describing the work of the World Health Organization Regional Office for Europe in developing a European strategy and action plan for migrant health providing advocacy, guidance and support to EU Member States in order to analyse health service preparedness, response and capacity to manage migration.

The second chapter focuses on the Migrant Integration Policy Index (MIPEX), an instrument for measuring integration policies across a range of countries. The author describes MIPEX's historical and ongoing relevance and explains the reasons behind its development. It also describes methodological aspects, including how MIPEX was developed, which categories of migrants and countries were studied, how policies are defined and how data is collected and analysed in the instrument. The chapter also presents descriptive results of the analysis and highlights insightful policy comparisons between groups of countries.

Chapter 3 focuses on recent context and commitments on the topic of migrant health. It discusses European policy in relation to the migration health framework, highlighting global policies on migrants in relation to the 2030 Sustainable Development Goals. The chapter explores the role of the Global Consultations on Migration Health organized by International Organisation for Migration and World Health Organisation and some important instruments that have been adopted in the European Union and in Member States as a meaningful platform for multi-sectoral dialogue and political commitment to enhance the health of migrants.

The fourth and fifth chapters focus on migrant and refugee health policy in Portugal. Chapter 4 emphasizes migration in the context of changing live-birth statistics, deaths and annual population estimates, and covers some important national legislation and public policy instruments to promote health equity of migrants. It also describes important innovative projects implemented within the High Commission for Migration mandate and designed to address health inequity, including the creation of national and local support centres for migrant integration, among others.

Chapter 5 offers an overview of the reception of asylum seekers and refugees in Portugal. It provides an analysis of the changing data relating to numbers of migrants seeking humanitarian protection in the country. The chapter examines the psychological, social and physical health of different groups of refugees and asylum seekers, as well as some of the primary challenges faced by them to accessing healthcare in Portugal, based on the experience of the Portuguese Refugee Council.

Chapter 6 returns to the European context and focuses on the challenges and barriers that asylum seekers and migrants face to access adequate health services. The chapter presents the results of interviews and focus groups conducted in ten European countries with healthcare professionals and managers working in centres for refugees and asylum seekers, in primary care services and hospitals. The author discusses the importance of different phases in migration trajectory - arrival, transit and destination phases-, in relation to migrant health, and concludes that lack of migrant-friendly health systems is an important factor impacting health service access and quality of care for refugees and asylum seekers.

The seventh chapter considers the impact of administrative structure, influence of stakeholders, politics and media on design and implementation of health policies for migrants in European countries. The chapter emphasises how attitudes towards migration are shaped and led by multiple factors, including societal challenges, political contexts and media discussions, beyond adherence to human rights. The author briefly outlines four case studies in European countries: Germany, The Netherlands, Spain and United Kingdom. The author concludes that it is imperative to understand policies and implementation of migrant access to healthcare in this broader context in order to effectively improve migrant health.

Chapter 8 focuses on the migrant health in the context of fundamental human rights, equity for migrants in healthcare and integration into host countries. The authors document the evidence on the links between health indicators and indicators of integration. In addition, the chapter examines health effects of different phases of migration, emphasizing the need to appreciate migrants as a heterogeneous population. It also highlights that collaboration and coordination between the countries, the different public sectors, the private organizations and the civil society is crucial in the context of migrant health. Focusing more on migrant health in research, policy and practice will help developing better health programs for the whole population.

The ninth chapter explores the migration phenomenon in Norway taking a historical perspective and considering when and why different migrant groups arrived in the country. The author considers that migration demography research has often overlooked health research, highlighting that the term "migrant" refers to complex subgroups of populations worldwide and emphasizing migration as a dynamic process. The author also uses data to dispel some popular migrant health myths. The chapter concludes that solutions to improve migrant health must involve migrants, empower all healthcare users and be driven by insightful research.

Chapter 10 documents the current knowledge and evidence on migrants' health, focusing on the Portuguese context. It takes a brief overview of the migrant health policies in Portugal and provides an analysis of the national research data on the general health status of migrants during the migration process and access to and use of health services. The authors highlight the influence of social determinants in health using data from community-based studies. The chapter concludes by reflecting on possible future research directions generating evidence to inform impactful policy and actions for reducing migrant health inequalities.

This book is intended for readers from all areas devoted to the health of migrants. We hope the reader learns as much as the participants in the seminar from the scientific and policy contributions. Several challenges emerged from the discussion, and constitute seeds for further work. We expect this book to be truly a beginning to provoke shared discussion, and that researchers, practitioners, policy makers and communities will find areas to inspire their interests, stimulate their thinking and expand their practice.

CHAPTER 1

The policy and politics of migrants and health: European view

SANTINO SEVERONI

Coordinator Public Health and Migration Division of Policy and Governance for Health and Well-being, WHO Regional Office for Europe

PALMIRA IMMORDINO

Technical Officer, Public Health and Migration Division of Policy and Governance for Health and Well-being, WHO Regional Office for Europe

The number of international migrants escaping from conflict and war, natural or manmade disaster, or as a result of financial crises and climate changes reached globally 244 million in 2015, a 41 per cent increase compared to 2000[1]. Long-term globalization, unequal developmental patterns and forced migration has led to an unpreceded growth of people on the move. As a result, worldwide at end of 2016, 22.5 million people were refugees, 40.3 million were internally displaced, and 2.8 million were asylum-seekers[2] with increasing numbers of unaccompanied minors, families with young children, pregnant women and elderly.

The health of migrants and health matters associated with migration are crucial public health challenges faced by governments and societies. In particular, health systems in receiving countries have to ensure adequate

[1] https://gmdac.iom.int/data-and-analysis-search

[2] http://www.unhcr.org/5943e8a34.pdf

living conditions for migrating populations in order to protect and promote their health. Many countries are well prepared to receive this large influx of migrants. However, the significant rise of influxes has called for an urgent coordinated response to address both the short- and the long-term implications of this phenomenon, as the health of mobile populations cannot be separated from the health of the rest of the population.

Looking at the European dimension of the phenomenon, the European Region has seen increasing arrivals since 2011[3], with over 1 million refugees and migrants arriving to the European Region throughout 2015. Similar trends in other regions, Eastern Mediterranean countries hosted 4.2 million refugees counties in Africa, the Americas, the Western Pacific, and South-East Asia have also seen a rise in a number of economic and other types of migrants.

According to the latest updates [4], 157,352 were the arrivals to Europe in 2017 and among those, 148,822 by sea and 8,530 by land. 2,793 dead missing people were registered. In 2016, 387,895 arrivals were registered in Europe and out of those 5,143 were dead or missing. Only in the European Region there are about 77 million international migrants, which represent 8% of its population[5].

The migrant population in the European Region comprises a heterogeneous population, composed of diverse and overlapping groups such as refugees, asylum seekers, labour migrants, undocumented migrants, etc. Therefore, governments and societies need also to take into consideration that health systems need to be prepared and adapted adequately to respond to the diverse health needs of this heterogeneous group.

The seven largest refugee populations are in Turkey, Pakistan, Lebanon, Iran, Ethiopia, Jordan, and Kenya, respectively. Together, these countries host more than half the world's refugees[6].

Countries including the European countries are going through an unprecedented situation which does not represent a humanitarian crisis in our Region, but a crisis of humanity. It is estimated that there will be

[3] http://ec.europa.eu/eurostat/statistics-explained/index.php/Migration_and_migrant_population_statistics

[4] http://data2.unhcr.org/en/situations/mediterranean

[5] http://www.euro.who.int/__data/assets/pdf_file/0004/197113/EHR2012-Eng.pdf

[6] http://data.unhcr.org/syrianrefugees/regional.php

over 200 million migrants by 2050[7]: as long as conflicts, violence and natural disasters persist, migration will be ever present.

Although migration is not a new phenomenon, international interest in the relationship between the policy and politics and the public health aspect of migration has received renewed attention due to the current migration flow that European countries are facing since almost ten years.

It has long been acknowledged that migration is a multi-sectoral agenda: dealing with the complex and multifaceted dynamics of migration requires a multi-sectoral approach being the health sector influenced by non-health sectors and policies (i.e. Ministries of Interior, Labour, Social Affairs, Foreign Affairs, and Education).

Governments are now starting to acknowledge that none health policies have more impact on the health of migrants than health policies.

Ensuring that refugees and migrants enjoy the highest attainable standard of physical and mental health is fundamental for the protection and promotion of human rights. These notions formed the basis for the Resolution WHA61.17 on the Health of Migrants[8]; endorsed by the Sixty-first World Health Assembly (WHA) in May 2008 and on 29 May 2017, the 70th World Health Assembly endorsed the Resolution on "Promoting the Health of Refugees and Migrants"[9]. The Resolution was co-sponsored by 14 countries; Argentina, Colombia, Ecuador, Greece, Haiti, Italy, Luxembourg, Mexico, Panama, Philippines, Portugal, Switzerland, Thailand, Zambia.

In the WHO European Region, the European health policy framework Health 2020[10] is fully in line with those concepts to: improve health and well-being across the entire Region; tackle health inequities within and between countries; address all determinants of health and invest in upstream approaches; support and protect vulnerable groups; prevent and control communicable and non-communicable diseases; and ensure sustainable, universal, and equitable people-centered health systems.

[7] https://esa.un.org/unpd/wpp/

[8] http://apps.who.int/iris/bitstream/10665/23533/1/A61_R17-en.pdf

[9] http://www.who.int/migrants/about/framework_refugees-migrants.pdf

[10] http://www.euro.who.int/__data/assets/pdf_file/0011/199532/Health2020-Long.pdf?ua=1

Guided by those principles, the WHO Regional Office for Europe in 2012 established with the financial support from the Ministry of Health of Italy the project Public Health Aspects of Migration in Europe (PHAME). The project has been built up on four areas of work: technical assistance; health information and evidence; advocacy and communication; and policy development. PHAME aimed at providing technical assistance and policy advice to countries receiving large influxes of refugees and migrants.

Since 2015, the Regional Office for Europe has scaled up its support to Member States on health and migration, given the increase of arrivals to the European Region and during the last three years, assessment missions have been conducted jointly with the Ministries of Health in Albania, Bulgaria, Cyprus, the Former Yugoslav Republic of Macedonia, Greece, Hungary, Italy, Malta, Portugal, Serbia and Spain with the aim to analyze the health-system preparedness, response and capacity to cope with the public health challenges posed by large-scale arrivals of refugees and migrants. As a result of those missions, it has been realized that all the assessment toolkits available were not addressing the needs to focus on the implications of large-scale migration movements to the health-system capacity[11]. Based on this evidence, the first toolkit for assessing health system capacity to manage large influxes of refugee asylum seekers and migrants[12] has been developed and the Regional Office for Europe has received requests to conduct similar exercises in Germany, Romania, Slovakia and to assess again the situation in Greece. The project has focused on strengthening the health-system capacity to protect the health of refugees, migrants and host communities; promoting immediate life-saving health interventions, as well as migrant-sensitive health policies; improving the quality of health services delivered and optimizing the utilization of health structures and resources in transit and destination countries.

The Regional Office for Europe has also strengthened collaboration with other United Nations (UN) agencies in order to provide clear

[11] http://www.euro.who.int/__data/assets/pdf_file/0018/325611/Toolkit-assessing-HS-capacity-manage-large-influxes-refugees-asylum-seekers-migrants.pdf?ua=1

[12] http://www.euro.who.int/__data/assets/pdf_file/0018/325611/Toolkit-assessing-HS-capacity-manage-large-influxes-refugees-asylum-seekers-migrants.pdf

guidance to countries in key areas, such as immunization for refugees, asylum seekers and migrants; mental health and psychosocial support. Therefore, policy briefs have been developed on different aspects of migrant health (communicable diseases, mental health, and environmental health).

Improving the availability of good quality data on public health and migration is essential in order to develop evidence-informed policies and interventions. With this regard, the Regional Office for Europe has published reviews of the evidence available on priority public health and migration issues: immunization services; maternal health care; definitions of "migrant" and their application on the access of migrants to health care; mental health; health status for labour migrants; health status for refugees and asylum seekers; health status for undocumented migrants.

Advocating for public health and migration in the European Region has been identified as another key area of work. Advocating and effectively communicating means sharing and making open access and available from any geographical location the best knowledge and training, as well as promoting best available evidence, good practices and evidence-informed approaches on migrant health. This cannot be done without engaging key stakeholders and building their capacity utilizing pre-existing training materials developing new resources to address the needed technical, logistical, operational and political support regarding migrants' health issues.

With the wider objective to transform a need into an opportunity to act, the Regional Office for Europe has worked on the policy development of Member States with regards to migration and health

The Regional Office for Europe has been taking the leading role, scaling up its activities on migration and health across European region. Following a technical briefing on the margins of the 64th session of the WHO Regional Committee for Europe (RC64), a ministerial lunch was held at RC65 to exchange views with Member States to prepare the ground and documentation for a formal discussion at RC66. It was emphasized that the Regional Committee should discuss the health and public health aspects of refugees and migrants and consider if there are any other aspects of migration where it can play a useful role, while staying within its mandate. As a result, a High-level Meeting on Refugee and Migrant Health was organized, with the aim of continuing the discussion towards a common public health understanding of the issues relating to migration and health within the Region, and for considering best policies and public health responses. An outcome document was discussed, which identified an agreed rationale, agenda and framework for collaborative action for addressing the health needs of refugees and migrant populations across the WHO European Region: the reviewed interest of countries participating to the High level meeting has been accompanied by requests for addressing the complexity of refugee and migrant movements from health perspective, as shown by the adoption of the first ever Strategy and action plan for refugee and migrant health in the WHO European Region[13], September last year as an attempt to find cross-border and collective solutions.

During the process of development of the European strategy and action plan, an inter-agency consultation was organized at the Regional Office for Europe to discuss the draft, with the aim to come up with a coherent document that is embraced and in line with the priorities of other partner agencies. It was stressed during the meeting the need to come up with a multi-agency approach to support the implementation of the action plan. Responding to the migration crisis, inter-agency collaboration has been strengthened among UN Agencies and other international organizations in order to bring coherence to the international efforts in this area. In particular, the Regional Office for Europe has established a collaborative action on migration and health leading to the development of draft framework of priorities and guiding principles to promote the health of refugees and migrants, which has been submitted to WHA70 as per previous discussion at the Executive Board last January 2017 and participated at the WHO-IOM 2nd Global Consultation in Colombo, Sri Lanka, in March 2017, and at the drafting of the Colombo statement through the drafting steering committee. The Colombo Statement is in line with the European strategy and action plan, as well as with the Resolution on "Promoting the Health of Refugees and Migrants", endorsed during the 70th World Health Assembly.

With the Knowledge Hub on Health and Migration, a new critical tool to the work on migration and health issues has been added: the Knowledge Hub on Health and Migration is an example of how The Region is

[13] http://www.euro.who.int/__data/assets/pdf_file/0004/314725/66wd08e_MigrantHealthStrategyActionPlan_160424.pdf

responding to the need for an educational institute devoted to international migration and public health. It will equip the global migration sphere with the evidence and data necessary to inform professionals and press, to back up responsible arguments with facts and numbers, and disseminate the right and formulated information to contribute to an informed-discussion on health and migration and evidence-based interventions.

Grounded in the European health policy framework, Health 2020, as well as the 2030 Agenda for Sustainable Development and the Strategy and Action Plan for Refugee and Migrant health, the objective of the Knowledge Hub is to provide a scientific and capacity-building forum to develop and improve public policies and interventions to address the health needs of migrants and the public health implications of migration in the WHO European Region. The expertise front-line European countries' officials in addressing migrant healthcare was a learning opportunity for the world and the organization of the first Summer School on Refugee and Migrant Health in July 2017, one of the flagship activities of the Knowledge Hub, was a response to the increasing need for knowledge exchange, discussion and inter-country collaboration.

Despite the complexity and political sensitivity around this topic, European countries are largely contributing and shaping the policy agenda at the global. The way forward is the development of a global action plan on the health of refugees and migrants, for submission to WHA in 2019, ensuring that health is highly taken into consideration within the global compact on refugees, and the global compact for safe, orderly and regular migration.

References

Data and Analysis [Internet]. IOM's Global Migration Data Analysis Centre. Available from: https://gmdac.iom.int/data-and-analysis-search

United Nations High Commissioner for Refugees. Global trends - Forced displacement in 2016 [Internet]. Geneva: UNHCR; 2017 p. 1-71. Available from: http://www.unhcr.org/5943e8a34.pdf

Eurostat, Statistics Explained. Migration and migrant population statistics from: http://ec.europa.eu/eurostat/statistics-explained/index.php/Migration_and_migrant_population_statistics

Mediterranean Situation [Internet]. Operational Portal – Refugee Situations. Available from: http://data2.unhcr.org/en/situations/mediterranean

World Health Organization Regional Office for Europe. The European health report 2012 Charting the way to well-being [Internet]. Copenhagen: World Health Organization Regional Office for Europe; 2013 p. 1-142. Available from: http://www.euro.who.int/__data/assets/pdf_file/0004/197113/EHR2012-Eng.pdf

Syria Regional Refugee Response [Internet]. Available from: http://data.unhcr.org/syrianrefugees/regional.php

United Nations of the Department of Economic and Social Affairs, Population Division, 2017 Revision of World Population Prospects from: https://esa.un.org/unpd/wpp/

World Health Organization. Health of Migrants [Internet]. 2008 p. 1-3. Available from: http://apps.who.int/iris/bitstream/10665/23533/1/A61_R17-en.pdf

World Health Organization. Promoting the health of refugees and migrants [Internet]. 2017 p. 1-4. Available from: http://www.who.int/migrants/about/framework_refugees-migrants.pdf

World Health Organization Regional Office for Europe. Health 2020 - A European policy framework and strategy for the 21st century [Internet]. Copenhagen: World Health Organization Regional Office for Europe; 2013 p. 1-182. Available from: http://www.euro.who.int/__data/assets/pdf_file/0011/199532/Health2020-Long.pdf?ua=1

World Health Organization Regional Office for Europe. Toolkit for assessing health system capacity to manage large influxes of refugees, asylum-seekers and migrants (2016) from: http://www.euro.who.int/__data/assets/pdf_file/0018/325611/Toolkit-assessing-HS-capacity-manage-large-influxes-refugees-asylum-seekers-migrants.pdf?ua=1

World Health Organization Regional Office for Europe. Toolkit for assessing health system capacity to manage large influxes of refugees, asylum-seekers and migrants [Internet]. Copenhagen: World Health Organization; 2016 p. 1-49. Available from: http://www.euro.who.int/__data/assets/pdf_file/0018/325611/Toolkit-assessing-HS-capacity-manage-large-influxes-refugees-asylum-seekers-migrants.pdf

World Health Organization Regional Office for Europe. Strategy and action plan for refugee and migrant health in the WHO European Region [Internet]. Copenhagen: World Health Organization; 2016 p. 1-29. Available from: http://www.euro.who.int/__data/assets/pdf_file/0004/314725/66wd08e_MigrantHealthStrategyActionPlan_160424.pdf

CHAPTER 2

The Migrant Integration Policy Index (MIPEX) Health strand: what it is and what it can tell us

DAVID INGLEBY

University of Amsterdam, Netherlands

1. Background to the MIPEX Health strand

a. History of the project

The Migrant Integration Policy Index (MIPEX) is an instrument for measuring integration policies across a range of countries, which has been expanded and implemented at four-yearly intervals since 2004 (see Table 1).

Currently, the project is administered by the Migration Policy Group (MPG) and the Barcelona Centre for International Affairs (CIDOB). This chapter describes the development and implementation of the eighth MIPEX strand, concerning Health, which was undertaken between 2013 and 2016 by a consortium drawn from the EQUI-HEALTH project of the International Organization for Migration (IOM), the EU COST Action IS1103 'ADAPT' (Adapting European Health Systems to Diversity), and the MPG. Financial support was provided by the EC, the IOM and other donors: altogether, some 150 experts from 40 countries collaborated in the project. The data were published on the MIPEX website in June 2015, followed by a Summary Report (1) and in 2017 by 34 Country Reports on the website of the EQUI-HEALTH project.[14]

[14] http://equi-health.eea.iom.int/index.php/migrant-health/milestones-and-deliverables-mh

Table 1. Successive rounds of the MIPEX survey

Date	Countries added	Strands added
2004[15]	EU15	Labour Market Inclusion, Family Reunion, Long Term Residence, Naturalization, Anti-Discrimination
2007	Ten more EU countries plus Canada, Norway and Switzerland	Political Participation
2011	Two more EU countries plus Australia, Japan, New Zealand, Serbia, South Korea and the USA	Education
2015	Croatia, Iceland and Turkey (Serbia dropped) *Total countries: 38*	Health *Total strands: 8*

In recent years there has been growing realisation of the importance of health as an aspect of integration. "Illness exacerbates marginalisation and marginalisation exacerbates illness, creating a downward spiral" (2). Health equity requires that the interests of migrants and their descendants should be taken into account not only in health services, but in all aspects of national policy that affect their health; successful integration policies reduce health threats to migrants and empower them to make optimal use of health services. Regrettably, however, policies to further health equity for migrants have lagged behind in many countries.

Like the other strands of MIPEX, the Health strand provides benchmarks that will enable countries to identify the most urgent weaknesses requiring attention and to compare their own progress with that of others. It is important to note that the instrument measures *relative*, not *absolute* standards of health care: provision is regarded as 'equitable' if it is not inferior to that offered to non-migrants, even if the standard offered to both may be less than optimal. In some situations, equity means treating migrants the same as non-migrants, but it also means treating them differently when this is called for.

[15] Under the title *The European Civic Citizenship and Inclusion Index.*

b. Why is it necessary to measure policies?

The first international conference on Migration and Health took place in The Hague in 1983 (3). Since that time, an increasing amount of research has been carried out on health risks for migrants, measures taken to counter these, access to health care and efforts to adapt services to the needs of migrants. Unfortunately, studies tend to cover different selections of countries and topics; they are not coordinated or harmonised with each other. A collection of instruments, however large, does not make an orchestra. Researchers often duplicate each other's efforts, at the same time leaving large gaps. Moreover, because of the different concepts, criteria and methods used, it is difficult to compare countries with each other.

What is required is a standardised method for describing policies, to be administered as comprehensively as possible. As with other aspects of integration, many different indicators need to be taken into account; yet in order to facilitate comparisons, they have to be reduced to a manageable number of dimensions. Qualitative information therefore has to be transformed into quantitative data, which is a familiar task for policy researchers. Scale construction is carried out by identifying a group of indicators measuring to some extent the same thing and adding them together, preferably weighting them according to their importance.

Using many indicators makes much more accurate comparisons possible. Consider, for example, the many international studies that have been carried out on the access of undocumented migrants (UDMs) to health care – some of which even cover all EU Member States. Most countries are classified as granting UDMs only 'emergency care'. But what does this mean in practice? Who decides what an 'emergency' is, and how much individual discretion is involved? Does the patient have to pay, and if so, how high are the fees? Are there explicit exemptions for those unable to pay, and are they easy to claim? Are there groups (such as children) or conditions (such as infectious diseases) to which the 'emergency' criterion does not apply? A simple all-or-nothing classification will not capture these nuances; in MIPEX, all of them are taken into account.

The question of weighting, however, is more difficult. Ideally the researcher needs to know how important a given indicator is for achieving equity. However, this cannot be determined without knowing the context: where the migrant population contains many children, policies on child health will be important; where many migrants are poor, affordability will be crucial. Some things considered important may not be so in practice, and vice versa. Because there is no reliable way of weighting the importance of items *a priori*, MIPEX uses a large number of indicators (38 in the Health strand, grouped into 23 questions), on the principle that errors of weighting or measurement will tend to cancel each other out. Although such a scale may give a useful indication of what it is supposed to measure, it can never reach the degree of precision required, for example, in the natural sciences. For this reason, the results from MIPEX are reported only in terms of a country's ranking on a five-point ordinal scale, each division corresponding as far as possible to an equal number of countries.

c. Choice of issues to be studied

Some issues regarding migrant health are by definition important: for example, to receive treatment in a health facility, a migrant must have access to it, and if communication is impossible because of language barriers, the quality of treatment will suffer. However, other barriers to equitable care for migrants are less self-evident; they have been identified on the basis of experience accumulated over the years by health professionals and migrants. Consensus over the issues that are important is not complete, but in a comparative content analysis of six publicly available approaches to 'organizational responsiveness to diversity' drawn from the USA, Australia and Europe, Seeleman et al. (4) found a great deal of agreement.

There is a particularly strong tradition of work on diversity and health in the USA, going back to the Civil Rights Movement and Civil Rights Act of 1964. Then, the concern was not so much with migrants as with minorities – though these groups overlap and the problems they experience can be similar, though seldom identical. A milestone in this work was the publication of the *National Standards for Culturally and Linguistically Appropriate Services (CLAS) in Health and Health Care* by the Office of Minority Health (5).

On the other side of the Atlantic, the Council of Europe (CoE) has published two sets of recommendations (6,7), based – like the CLAS standards – on extensive reviews of research and consultations with experts and civil society organisations. The 2011 recommendations were particularly detailed: it was on the basis of this work that the issues to be measured by the MIPEX Health strand were selected. The 2011 document contained 14 recommendations, explained in 23 guidelines, divided into 6 categories.

1. *Improving knowledge about migrants and their situation*
2. *Researching migrants' state of health*
3. *Entitlement to health service provision*
4. *Accessibility of the health system*
5. *Quality of health services for migrants*
6. *General measures to promote change.*

MIPEX strands contain only four dimensions, but this discrepancy was easily resolved by subsuming the first and second categories under the last. The four sections in the Health strand questionnaire initially contained 6 questions each, with one or more indicators per question. One question had to be eliminated for methodological reasons, so the final scale had 23 questions. These were scored on a three-point ordinal scale with the following levels:

0 = no effort to avoid inequities
50 = a defined intermediate position
100 = equitable or nearly equitable policies

Items within each section were averaged, as well as all the items in the questionnaire. The sections were as follows:

Table 2. Sections of the MIPEX Health strand and their content

	Topic	Content
A	**Legal entitlements to health care**	Conditions and extent of coverage, as well as administrative obstacles to obtaining legal entitlements (documents that are hard for migrants to obtain, discretionary judgements).
B	**Accessibility of services**	Information for migrants and service providers on entitlements and use of health services; health promotion for migrants; use of mediators to facilitate access; threat of reporting to authorities.
C	**Appropriateness and acceptability of services**	Availability of interpretation, standards for 'cultural competence' or 'diversity sensitivity' and availability of training in these, migrant involvement in service delivery, diversity in the health workforce, adaptation of diagnostic and treatment methods.
D	**'Flanking measures' to improve A-C**	Data collection and research, 'health in all policies' approach, 'whole organisation' approach, leadership by government, involvement of stakeholders and consultation with migrant organisations.

'Access' is a very broad notion, containing many components. In MIPEX, as in the CoE recommendations, a fundamental distinction is made between legal entitlements (Section A) and practical barriers making it harder for migrants to reach the appropriate service provider (Section B). 'Entitlement' determines the affordability of care: whether migrants are allowed to join the country's system of risk-sharing, whether tax-based or insurance-based. Countries sometimes give good entitlements but set up administrative obstacles to exercising them; these reduce the score in Section A for entitlements. For example, UDMs in Portugal can receive free treatment if they are in 'financial need', but the procedure for proving such need presents obstacles that are difficult for such migrants to surmount.

Precise details of individual questions and the rules for scoring them, as well as some analyses, can be found in the Summary Report (1). Raw scores are available on the MIPEX website (mipex.eu), though not in an easily readable form. The numerical database for the Health strand and the latest version of the questionnaire can be downloaded from the IOM's

EQUI-HEALTH website.[16] Detailed Country Reports are also available there, describing the background to the scores and providing a précis of the questionnaire responses (also mentioning recent developments where appropriate).

2. Development of the instrument

a. Categories of migrants studied

MIPEX focuses on third country nationals (TCNs), not only because their needs may be different from those of EU/EFTA migrants, but also because they are subject to different legislation. In the Health strand, the first category of TCNs is labelled 'legal migrants', referring primarily to those with a residence permit for work reasons. (Family members, students, retirees and recognised refugees are also 'legal migrants', but different rules often apply to them.) Asylum seekers form the second category, and UDMs the third.

Separate scores for each of these categories of migrant are given only for section A. However, all three groups are asked about separately within some questions in the other sections; the answers contribute to the scores and are described in the Country Reports.

Although MIPEX focuses on migrants, many of the issues studied are also relevant to non-migrant members of ethnic minorities (whether indigenous or formed by migration), as well as to EU/EFTA migrants. Descendants of migrants, like migrants who have obtained citizenship, may have the same legal entitlements as non-migrants, but they can experience other types of inequity; the same may be true for indigenous minorities. EU migrants should also enjoy better entitlements than TCNs, but they may experience barriers of accessibility (B) and lack of responsiveness to their needs (C). Therefore, tackling the inequities that have been identified for TCNs can at the same time contribute to solving many of the problems experienced by ethnic minorities and EU/EFTA migrants.

b. Countries studied

Data for the Health strand were collected from the 38 countries in MIPEX, as well as the Former Yugoslav Republic of Macedonia and Bosnia & Herzegovina. For the 'traditional countries of migration' (USA, Canada, Australia

[16] http://equi-health.eea.iom.int/index.php/migrant-health/milestones-and-deliverables-mh

and New Zealand), results were reported but not included in the statistical analyses, because the EQUI-HEALTH project included only the EU28, EEA (except Liechtenstein), Switzerland, FYR Macedonia, Bosnia & Herzegovina, and Turkey. Results from Japan and South Korea were reported on the MIPEX website but not included in any analyses, because of certain difficulties in applying concepts to those settings.

For the purpose of defining TCNs, Norway, Iceland and Switzerland were classified together with EU28 countries; within these countries, policies on health care coverage for each others' citizens are largely harmonised.

c. Definition of policy

In contrast to some other MIPEX strands, in which all policies are laid down in national laws, the Health strand considers all the levels at which health policy may be made. These include national, regional, or local governments; service provider organisations; professional bodies; and universities or medical schools. Different issues are often regulated by different policy-making bodies. NGOs are considered part of the health system if their activities received a government subsidy.

The fact that there may be regional differences in policy in some countries is dealt with in MIPEX by selecting two migrant-rich regions and amalgamating the results from them. In the Health strand, respondents were asked to apply the same principle whenever policies differed markedly within a country, focussing on those found in 'migrant-rich' areas. It should therefore be borne in mind that the high scores obtained in some countries may not be applicable outside such areas.

d. Formulating and refining the questions

Development of the questionnaire was carried out within the ADAPT project, an EU-financed network of 130 experts on diversity and health with members in 30 countries. Between 2011 and 2016 the network held 45 meetings with 25-30 participants each time, seven of which were devoted to developing the Health strand questionnaire. About 40 members were involved in these meetings, which were also attended by representatives of IOM and MPG.

The task involved converting the items in the CoE's 2011 recommendations into a 24-item questionnaire, constructed according to the MIPEX format and conventions. In 10 questions, two or more indicators were combined. Clear rules for coding the information collected were formulated; category boundaries were then adjusted to ensure a reasonable spread of answers over all response categories. Some questions had to be 'fine-tuned' to improve item-total correlations, or when experts reported difficulties in answering them. For one question it proved impossible to find a satisfactory formulation, so it was removed.

e. Data collection

After the questionnaire had been finalised, data were collected by experts in each country, specially appointed for this purpose by IOM and approved by MPG. Some experts also collected information for other MIPEX strands. This work was financed by IOM as part of the EQUI-HEALTH project, though some countries provided data on a voluntary basis. In each country at least two experts were appointed, one of whom acted as Peer Reviewer. In some countries larger teams were often formed, in which all members had their work checked by at least one other member. IOM and MPG also performed final checks. To ensure independence, experts affiliated to government departments were not employed.

Raw scores and original questionnaires are available on the MIPEX website (mipex.eu), though not in an easily readable form. To supplement this, detailed Country Reports have been published on the IOM website[17] describing the background to the scores and providing a précis of the questionnaire responses, also mentioning recent developments where appropriate. The numerical database for the Health strand and the latest version of the questionnaire can be downloaded from the same site.

3. Internal analysis of the instrument

a. Statistical properties

The internal consistency of the whole scale is good (Cronbach's alpha = 0.86). Factor analysis (principal component extraction with promax rotation) revealed three main factors, accounting respectively for 23, 14 and 12 per cent of the variance. The questions loading highly on to Factor 1 comprised the whole of Sections C and D, with the exception of question

[17] http://equi-health.eea.iom.int/index.php/migrant-health/milestones-and-deliverables-mh

17 (on encouraging diversity in the workforce) in Section C. This question was most closely related to Factor 2, as were the first three questions of Section A (on legal rights to health care coverage for the three categories of migrants). This suggests that diversity in the workforce is seen more as a matter of equal access to employment than of improving 'sensitivity to diversity' – an interpretation backed up by the comments of some respondents. Factor 3 was the main contributor to the second three questions of Section A (on administrative barriers to exercising entitlement) and the whole of Section B (on the ease of reaching service providers). The exception was question 7 (provision of information to service providers). This question may have been uninformative because it did not distinguish between countries that provided little information to service providers because the rules were very simple, and those who did so despite the rules being very complicated.

b. What does internal analysis tell us about policy?

Total scores on the Health strand have quite a high correlation with the average of the other MIPEX strands ($r = .57, p < .01$ two-tailed). The strands that correlate most highly with Health are Political Participation, Education, Access to Nationality and Labour Market Mobility (all significant at $p < .01$ two-tailed). Family Reunion, Permanent Residence and Anti-Discrimination showed no significant correlations with Health. Concerning the separate sections within the Health strand:

Section A. As expected, entitlements in almost every country were best for legal migrants and worst for UDMs, with asylum seekers in between.

- In many countries health care coverage for legal migrants was remarkably incomplete. Often, participation in the country's national system of risk-sharing was granted to migrants only after a long stay in the country or on condition that they remained in employment – two problems already highlighted in the CoE's 2011 recommendations. There were even cases where migrants were required to contribute to the country's risk-sharing system through taxes, but not allowed to join it.
- Many countries restrict access to primary care for asylum seekers by applying rather loosely defined criteria of 'emergency', 'urgent' or 'essen-

tial' care, always involving a degree of administrative discretion that makes it difficult to know in advance whether seeking care will result in heavy expenses. Unfortunately, this is what the EU's Directive on standards (8) regards as an adequate level of basic health care, despite the clear consensus among public health experts that low-threshold access to affordable primary care is essential for maintaining health and reducing costs. (Denial of such access is also regarded by the United Nations as incompatible with the right to health (9)). The current law in Germany, which at present houses more asylum seekers than any other country in Europe, is therefore unfit for purpose (10).

- From many other studies it was expected that UDMs would generally have poor entitlements, often subject to discretionary judgements. Most countries provided only 'emergency care', with a wide range of variations in the conditions for receiving it (cf. section 1b above). Detailed results from the MIPEX survey are presented in the Summary Report (1) and in IOM Recommendations [11]. Legislation is in place in several countries to allow UDMs affordable access to non-emergency care, but access is often impeded by barriers of many kinds, including administrative obstacles to claiming coverage, discretionary judgements, and lack of information among service providers and UDMs about their rights and fear of being reported).

Section B. The results here often showed a shocking lack of information issued to both migrants and service providers about migrants' entitlements. (Indeed, even for our expert researchers it was sometimes a challenge to discover exactly what these entitlements were.) Because of this, many migrants probably end up paying more for their care than they need to, or forego needed treatment. Information about using health services, as well as health education and promotion, are also sparse. This is surprising, given the fact that web sites or mobile apps are an inexpensive way of making this information accessible to large numbers of migrants in many languages. Likewise, few countries offer mediators or 'patient navigators' to help migrants find their way into care.

Section C. A very wide range of differences was found in this section, which measures policies related to 'cultural competence' or 'diversity sensitivity'. Such concepts seem to be unheard of in the eight countries that score zero for this section; there, a 'one-size-fits-all' approach to health care delivery prevails. By contrast, policies in other countries are frequently concerned with diversity; the UK scores 92 out of a possible 100. Within this section, there is a high degree of intercorrelation between items (Cronbach's alpha = .87), as would indeed be expected from the above findings. Interestingly, the correlation between scores on A and C was low (r = .23, NS two-tailed): although these are extreme cases, it is possible to find countries scoring high on entitlements but low on 'diversity sensitivity' (France, Turkey), or vice versa (UK, USA).

Section D. An unexpected result was that scores on Section D, concerned with measures to achieve change, are only significantly associated with scores on Section C on adapting services to diversity ($r = .67, p < .01$ two-tailed). By contrast, there is no significant relation with Section A on entitlements. This suggests that policies to promote equity in migrant health care are mainly concerned with making services more responsive, rather than to improving entitlements. Perhaps it is not widely realised how serious the gaps in entitlements are; or perhaps there is simply widespread political reluctance to fill them.

4. Relation of scores to other variables

a. Background variables

Which features of a country are associated with strong or weak policies on health equity for migrants? This is a very important question for those concerned with improving these policies. Because the MIPEX Health strand has different sections (scales), which behave in significantly different ways, we need to examine both the total scores and the separate scales.

The correlation of selected country characteristics with Health Strand scores is shown in Table 3. ('PP' stands for 'purchasing power). Luxembourg has been removed from the sample as an outlier, because its GDP is 2.7 times higher than the EU average.[18]

[18] Slight discrepancies between the results reported here and those given in the Summary Report are due to the fact that only EU countries were analysed in that report, whereas these analyse the full EQUI-HEALTH sample of 34 countries.

Table 3. Correlations with country characteristics

Variable	Total	A	B	C	D
GDP per capita 2014 (PP adjusted)	.70**	.41*	.46**	.74**	.39**
Percentage of TCNs in population	.48**	.25	.28	.54**	.28
Health expenditure per capita (PP adjusted)	.72**	.47**	.52**	.73**	.36
Euro Health Consumer Index (EHCI)	.55**	.44*	.39*	.54**	.23
Average of other MIPEX scores	.57**	.36*	.44*	.51**	.41*
Insurance-based (1) or Tax-based (2) health system	.34	-.23	.31	.40*	.38*

However, many of these background variables are correlated with each other, some may be acting as confounders.

Table 4. Correlations among country characteristics

	GDP	Percentage of TCNs	Health expenditure per capita	ECHI	Other MIPEX strands
Percentage of TCNs	.67**				
Health expenditure PC	.95**	.73**			
EHCI	.80**	.59**	.83**		
Other MIPEX strands	.48**	.43*	.53**	.60**	
NHS Health system	.33	.25	.19	.21	.33

Stepwise multiple regression was carried out on the above country characteristics, yielding the following significant results:

Table 5. Regression of Health strand scores on country characteristics

Dependent variable	Independent variables	Standardized beta	Significance (p)	R^2 (adj.)
Total	Health expenditure per capita	.74	.000	.53
A	Health expenditure per capita Tax-based health system	.60 -.40	.000 .011	.38
B	Health expenditure per capita	.49	.005	.21
C	Health expenditure per capita	.74	.000	.53
D	Tax-based health system	.39	.032	.12

These results suggest that the most basic determinant of Health strand scores, except for D, is Health expenditure per capita. Countries that spend more on each inhabitant's health also tend to treat migrants more equitably. Conversely, shortage of funding for the health system is strongly associated with inequities for migrants. This is hardly a surprising finding.

The country's type of health system plays an unexpected role. Having a tax-based system has a negative influence on scale A (Entitlements), but a positive one on scale D (Measures to achieve change). The difference is a small one; the first one only achieves significance in a multivariate analysis using both health system and health expenditure as independent variables. It is often assumed that tax-based systems of coverage are in principle more equitable, but here we see that countries with such a system are more likely to exclude migrants from the system of coverage. These countries do pay more attention to achieving change (perhaps because central control tends to be stronger), but the change appears only to concern adaptations to service delivery, not entitlements (cf. above, section 3b).

It should be noted that using multiple regression with independent variables that correlate quite strongly with each other, especially when the sample size is fairly small, is not completely reliable; the above relationships will need further examination. There may also be many other variables that have significant relationships with Health strand scales – only a handful have been explored here. For example, we have not studied any relationships with political differences and public opinion.

b. Differences between groups of countries

1. Comparison between EU15 and EU13 countries

One of the most striking findings of this study was that whether a member state joined the EU before 2004 (EU15) or afterwards (EU13) is in itself a very strong predictor of Health strand scores. The difference is particularly large in relation to C (Responsiveness to diversity); this concept seems to be virtually unknown in most EU13 countries.

These differences cannot be explained away by the fact that Health expenditure per capita is also a major determinant of the scores, and EU15 countries have much higher expenditures than the EU13 (means = €2927 versus €1305). In a stepwise regression with Health expenditure per capita, EU15 versus EU13 and Tax-based health system as the independent variables, the following variables emerged as the most powerful (Table 6):

Table 6. Regression of Health strand scores on health expenditure, type of health system and date of accession to the EU[19]

Dependent variable	Independent variables	Standardized beta	Significance (p)	R^2 (adj.)
Total	EU15 versus EU13	.74	.000	.53
A	Health expenditure per capita Tax-based health system	.55 -.33	.002 .047	.34
B	EU15 versus EU13	.55	.002	.28
C	EU15 versus EU13	.67	.000	.43
D	Tax-based health system	.57	.001	.33

The influence of the type of health system on scales A and D is still found in this analysis (as it was in Table 5), but in the total score and scales B and C, date of accession forces health expenditure out of the equation. This suggests that over and above the economic differences between these

[19] Luxembourg was included in this analysis.

Figure 1. Mean scores for the EU15, EU13, and Traditional Countries of Migration (TCM; USA, Canada, Australia, New Zealand)

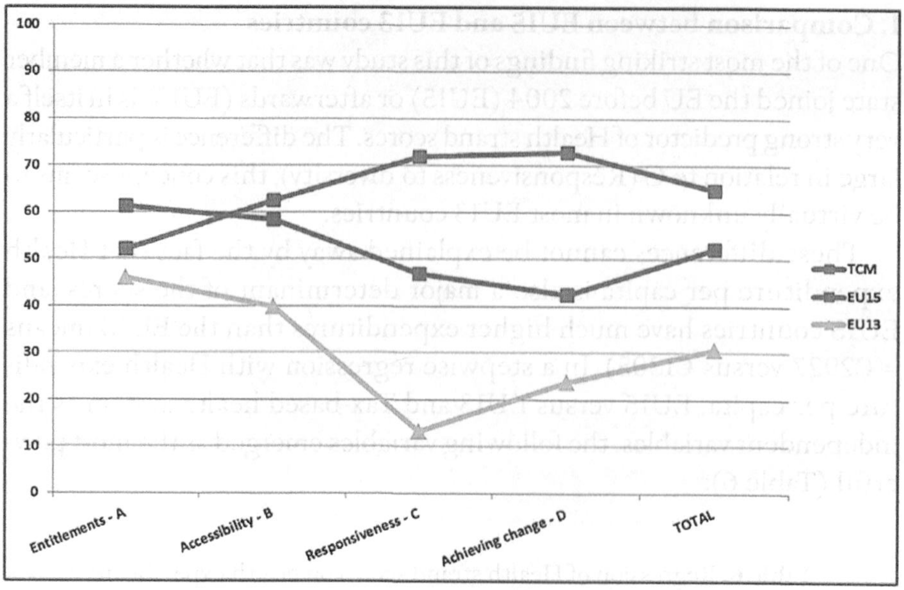

two groups of countries, there is some other factor (perhaps an ideological difference) hampering the development of equitable health policies for migrants in the EU13. More detailed investigation of this finding is required, which if valid has important implications for policy. Scores for the two groups of countries can be compared in Fig. 1 (above).

2. Comparison between EU15, EU13 and Traditional Countries of Migration

Comparing the EU13 with TCM is not very relevant, because migrant stock in these countries is very low (7%) compared with the EU15 and TCM (16% and 22%). GDP is also low in the EU13 (69), as against 129 for both the EU15 and TCM[20]. Europe has always been regarded as lagging behind in attention for health and diversity, but Figure 1 shows that as far as the EU15 is concerned, this is only true for scales C and D – not for A and B.

[20] 2014 figures, Eurostat figures (EU mean = 100); Luxembourg omitted as outlier.

Figure 2 shows entitlements in all countries for three types of migrant separately.

Figure 2. Entitlements (A) for different types of migrants in three groups of countries

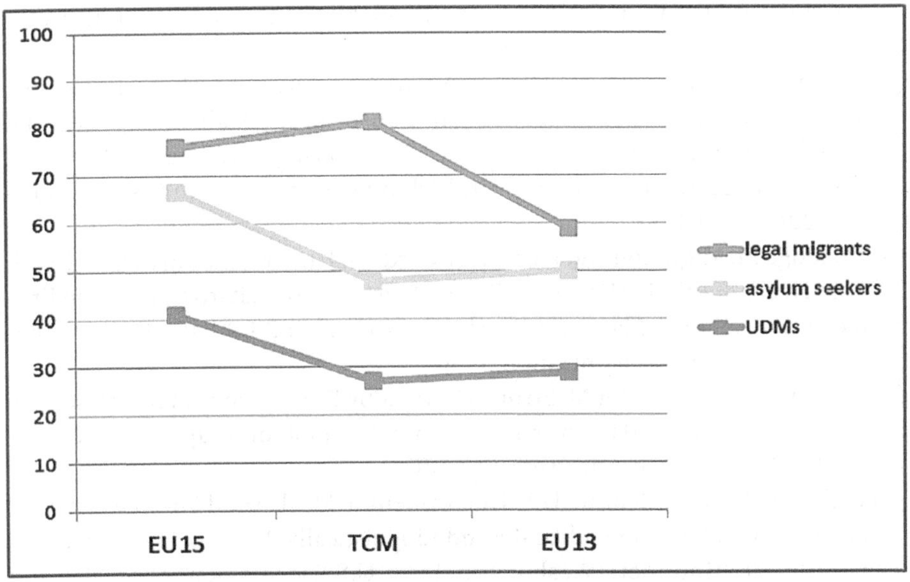

The interesting finding in this graph is that for legal migrants, entitlements are similar in the EU15 and TCM; but for asylum seekers and undocumented migrants, entitlements are better in the EU15 than in both the TCM and EU13, where they are at roughly the same level. For these two groups, humanitarian considerations play a greater role than for legal migrants; perhaps such considerations play a greater role in the EU15 than in the EU13 and TCM.

5. Conclusions

The MIPEX Health strand has yielded a large amount of data on policies affecting the health of migrants, which has already generated valuable insights into the nature and determinants of these policies. It is hoped that countries will make use of this information, as well as that in the individual

Country Reports, to compare their policies with those in other countries and to tackle weaknesses that have been identified.

References

(1) International Organization for Migration. Summary Report on the MIPEX Health Strand and Country Reports [Internet]. Geneva: International Organization for Migration; 2016 p. 1-124. Available from: https://publications.iom.int/system/files/mrs_52.pdf

(2) Ingleby D, Chimienti M, Hatziprokopiou P, Ormond M, de Freitas C. The role of health in integration. In: Fonseca ML, Malheiros J, editors. Social integration and mobility: education, housing and health IMISCOE Cluster B5 State of the art report. Lisbon: Centro de Estudos Geográficos; 2005. p. 101–37.

(3) Colledge M. Migration and Health: Towards an Understanding of the Health Care Needs of Ethnic Minorities. Proceedings of a Consultative Group on Ethnic Minorities (The Hague, Netherlands, November 28-30, 1983). Copenhagen: World Health Organization; 1986.

(4) Seeleman C, Essink-Bot M, Stronks K, Ingleby D. How should health service organizations respond to diversity? A content analysis of six approaches. BMC Health Services Research. 2015;15(1):510.

(5) Office of Minority Health - U.S. Department of Health and Human Services. National Standards for Culturally and Linguistically Appropriate Services in Health Care [Internet]. Washington, D.C.: U.S. Department of Health and Human Services; 2001 p. 1-132. Available from: https://minorityhealth.hhs.gov/assets/pdf/checked/finalreport.pdf

(6) Recommendation Rec(2006)18 of the Committee of Ministers to member states on health services in a multicultural society [Internet]. Council of Europe - Committee of Ministers. 2006. Available from: https://wcd.coe.int/ViewDoc.jsp?p=&Ref=Rec(2006)18&Sector=secCM&Language=lanEnglish&Ver=original&BackColorInternet=DBDCF2&BackColorIntranet=FDC864&BackColorLogged=FDC864&direct=true

(7) Recommendation CM/Rec(2011)13 of the Committee of Ministers to member states on mobility, migration and access to health care [Internet]. Council of Europe - Committee of Ministers. 2011 [cited 31 January 2018]. Available from: https://search.coe.int/cm/Pages/result_details.aspx?ObjectID=09000016805cbd6d

(8) Directive 2013/33/EU of the European Parliament and of the Council of 26 June 2013 laying down standards for the reception of applicants for international protection [Internet]. EUR-Lex Access to European Union law. 2013.

Available from: http://eur-lex.europa.eu/legal-content/EN/TXT/?uri=celex:32013L0033
(9) UN Committee on Economic, Social and Cultural Rights (CESCR). CESCR General Comment No. 3: The Nature of States Parties' Obligations (Art. 2, Para. 1, of the Covenant) [Internet]. 2018 p. 1-5. Available from: http://www.refworld.org/docid/4538838e10.html
(10) Bozorgmehr K, Razum O. Effect of Restricting Access to Health Care on Health Expenditures among Asylum-Seekers and Refugees: A Quasi-Experimental Study in Germany, 1994–2013. PLOS ONE. 2015;10(7):e0131483.
(11) International Organization for Migration. Equi-Health, Recommendations on access to health services for migrants in an irregular situation: an expert consensus [Internet]. Brussels: International Organization for Migration; 2016 p. 1-59. Available from: http://equi-health.eea.iom.int/images/Expert_consensus_Recommendations.pdf

CHAPTER 3

Factors to ensure equity in health for migrants in Europe

Federica Viello, Roumyana Petrova-Benedict, Isabelle Beauclercq, Elena Val
IOM, Migration Health Division, Brussels

Over 1 billion people in the world are migrants, or more than 1 in 7 people globally (1). The figure includes the stock of international migrants (people residing in a country other than their country of birth) whose number reached 244 million in 2015, an increase by 41 per cent since 2000, and around 740 million internal migrants (2). However, the proportion of international migrants in the world population is only slightly higher than that recorded over the past decades, at 3.2 per cent in 2013 compared to 2.8 per cent in 2000 (1).

In the European Union, the most relevant migration flows in 2000's were the Eastern enlargements in 2004 and 2007, causing substantial East-West migration flows as well as the 2008 financial crisis that induced a reduction of immigration into Europe, but at the same time to an increase in intra-European movements (3). While migrants from the Middle East, South East Asia, and Africa have been crossing the Mediterranean to reach Europe in growing numbers since 2011, 2015 marked the sharpest increase in arrivals to Europe (4). In 2015, the year with the highest number of people displaced by violence and conflicts since WWII, 1,046,599 migrants made their way to Europe, including 1,011,712 arrivals by sea, with Greece and Italy receiving the majority of migrants (857,363 and 153,842 arrivals respectively). The majority originated from the world's top refugees producing countries, principally Syria, Afghanistan and Iraq (4). however, out of the 65.6 million forcibly people displaced worldwide, Europe hosted the least percentage wise, 3.5 million asylum seekers and refugees, which corresponds to 0.68% of the European population (5)[21].

1. Migration Health Framework

The Resolution on the Health of Migrants endorsed by the World Health Assembly in May 2008 (6), called upon Member States to promote migrant-sensitive health policies and equitable access to health promotion, disease prevention and care, as well as encourage organisations to promote migrant health on the international agenda (7).

First WHO/IOM Consultation on Health of migrants, 2010

Following the Resolution on the Health of Migrants, IOM and World Health Organisation (WHO), in collaboration with the Ministry of Health and Social Policy of Spain, held a Global Consultation on Migration Health on 3-5 March 2010 in the context of the Spain's EU Presidency. The inputs and recommendations from the Consultation were aggregated into an Operational Framework to guide the action of stakeholders (6). It includes four priorities:

- Monitoring migrant health: strengthening knowledge on the health of migrants via research and information dissemination to ensure evidence-based programming and policy development
- Policy and Legal Framework: advocating for migrant inclusive health policies and programmes at national, regional and global levels, and assists in the development of policies to promote and protect the health of migrants.
- Migrant Sensitive Health System: delivering, facilitating and promoting equitable access to migrant-friendly and comprehensive health care services.

[21] http://www.unhcr.org/figures-at-a-glance.html

Partnerships, networks and multi-country frameworks: commitment to developing and strengthening multi-sectoral partnerships and coordination among member states, stakeholders and migrants (8).

2. Policies at global level

Recently, some key achievements in the recognition of the importance of the topic have been achieved whilst further spurring is remains key.

2030 Agenda Sustainable Development Goals[22]

The Sustainable Development Goals' (SDG) target 10.7 calls for orderly, safe, and responsible migration and mobility of people, including through implementation of planned and well-managed migration policies (9). In addition, the SDGs incites member states to achieve universal health coverage (target 3.8.) and emphasise the "leaving no one behind" principle. The targets endeavoured to be met for all nations and people and for all segments of society and, moreover to reach first those who are furthest behind (10). However, the interpretation of Universal Health Coverage as an overarching aspirational health goal, in many instances does not extend beyond coverage on the basis of citizenship (11).

Global Compacts on refugees and migrants

Health is missing among the "elements" of the Global Compacts on refugees and migrants. The Compacts, built upon the New York Declaration adopted on 19 September 2016, will set out a range of principles, commitments and understandings among Member States regarding international migration in all its dimensions (12).

Integrating health into the thematic sessions of the Global Compact on Migration, will allow Member States to formulate the needed actionable objectives. This in turn will assist in mainstreaming the migration health agenda in domains such as migration and development, global health, health security, occupational safety, disaster risk-reduction, climate and environmental change, and foreign policy (11).

[22] The Sustainable Development Goals are a universal call to action to end poverty, protect the planet and ensure that all people enjoy peace and prosperity.

140th WHO Executive Board

The WHO Executive Board at its 140th session in January 2017 requests WHO to prepare, in cooperation with Member States, IOM, UNHCR and other relevant stakeholders, a draft framework of priorities and guiding principles to promote the health of refugees and migrants, to be considered by the 70th World Health Assembly (13) and to make every possible effort, to ensure that health aspects are adequately addressed in the development of the global compact on refugees and the global compact for safe, orderly and regular migration (13).

Second IOM/WHO Global Consultation on Health of Migrants, 2017

In response to the renewed international attention to the topic of migration health, IOM, WHO and the Government of the Democratic Socialist Republic of Sri Lanka jointly organized the second Global Consultation on Migrant Health on 21-23 February 2017 to offer Member States and partners a meaningful platform for multi-sectoral dialogue and political commitment to enhance the health of migrants (14). Ministers and Government Representatives reaffirmed the enjoyment of the highest attainable standard of physical, mental, and social well-being is a fundamental right of every human being. They recognized that the enhancement of migrants' health status relies on an equitable and non-discriminatory access to health care and cross-border continuity of care at an affordable cost and that investment in migrant health provides positive dividends compared to public health costs due to exclusion and neglect. The importance of multi-sectoral coordination and inter-country engagement and partnership was also reaffirmed. They agreed to contribute to the formulation of a meaningful Global Compact on Safe, Orderly and Regular Migration (14,15).

Promoting the health of refugees and migrants, the World Health Assembly, 2017

In May 2017, the World Health Assembly endorsed the resolution 'Promoting the health of refugees and migrants'. The resolution encourages Member States to use the Framework of priorities and guiding principles to promote the health of refugees and migrants at all levels and to ensure that health is adequately addressed both in the Global Compact for Refugees (GCR) and the GCM.

Based on the Framework, to further provide health resources for the development of the draft GCM, WHO in close cooperation with IOM, ILO, OHCHR, UNAIDS, and other stakeholders, developed the "Proposed Health Component in the Global Compact for Safe, Orderly and Regular Migration". The document proposes eight actionable commitments and the means of implementation. Despite these promising developments, coordination and persistent advocacy is needed in order to include health in the final GCM in 2018.

3. Policies at EU level

At European level, some important instruments have been adopted during the past decade to promote the equity in health for migrants.

Minimum standards for the reception of asylum seekers

In 2003, in the light of the commitments arising from the Common European Asylum System[23], the European Commission (EC) urges Member States to harmonize the conditions for the reception of asylum seekers in the EU (16).

Through the Council Directive 2003/9/EC (re-casted in 2013 - 2013/33/EU), the EC defined minimum standards for the reception of asylum seekers. The Directive invites Member States to ensure an adequate standard of living and to ensure that applicants receive the necessary health care which shall include, at least, emergency care and essential treatment of illness (17).

The Portuguese EU Presidency

The Portuguese Presidency (July-December 2007) represented an important expression of political commitment to guaranteeing access to health for migrants. The conference "Health and Migration in the EU: Better health

[23] Since 1999 the EU has been working to create a Common European Asylum System and improve the legislative framework. In relation to the conditions of reception, the Reception Conditions Directive ensures that there are humane material reception conditions for asylum seekers across the EU and that the fundamental rights are fully respected. (European Commission, A common European Asylum System, Belgium, 2014.

for all in an inclusive society", held in September 2007, was an important event to discuss the health implications of migration (18). The Presidency, led a process of dialogue with Member States and other stakeholders aiming at progressively building a consensus in the EU on a common approach towards migrant health.

The impact of the Portuguese Presidency has been significant. In December 2007, the Employment, Social Policy, Health and Consumer Affairs (EPSCO) Council adopted the conclusions of the 'Health and Migration in the EU' Presidency Conference. The Council Conclusions invited European institutions and Member States to take action on the subject and integrate migrant health issues into health, employment, social and other national policies.

Portugal has continued to play a key role in spurring the development of the World Health Assembly Resolution "Promoting the health of refugees and migrants".

The debate on migration health and health inequalities was carried on by the Spanish Presidency (January-June 2010). The Council conclusions on Equity and Health in All Policies: Solidarity in Health invite the EU Member States and institutions to enhance public health capacities and promote equity in health across the different policy sectors and to aim at universal access to health care (18).

Resolution on reducing health inequalities in the EU

In 2011, the European Parliament (EP) approved a resolution which aimed at reducing health inequalities in the EU. On the basis of the universal values of human dignity, freedom, equality and solidarity, the resolution points to the need to maintain and improve universal access to healthcare systems and to affordable care. The resolution calls on the EC and Member States to ensure that the most vulnerable groups (including disadvantaged migrant groups, people belonging to ethnic minorities and undocumented migrants) are entitled to and are provided with equitable access to healthcare. The resolution underlined the importance of providing language mediation services and of developing training initiatives to enable health professionals to adopt an intercultural approach based on recognition of, and respect for, diversity and the needs of people from different geographical regions (19).

EU Action Plan on the Integration of Third-Country Nationals
More recently, the EU Action Plan on the Integration of Third-Country Nationals of June 2016 draw particular attention to the universal access to healthcare services. Recognizing that "ill health and lack of access to health services can be a fundamental and ongoing obstacle to integration", one of its priorities is to guarantee the access to adequate basic services such as housing and healthcare for third-country nationals (20).

European Pillar of Social Rights
The European Pillar of Social Rights, adopted by the EC in April 2017 covers important actions on the social determinants of health: the right to timely access to affordable, preventive and curative health care; children's right to affordable early childhood education and care; the right to adequate social protection regardless of the duration and type of employment relationships (21). This is a significant step toward the integration of migrants in the EU health systems; the principle 16 explicitly states that "everyone has the right to timely access to affordable, preventable and curative health care of good quality"[24].

Communication on the protection of children in migration
Given the increasing number of migrant children arriving in Europe in the last few years, the Communication from the EC to the EP and the Council on the protection of children in migration sets out a series of actions which need to be either taken or better implemented in order to ensure effective protection of children. Through this document, the EC expressed its commitment to ensure that the best interests of the child will be the primary consideration in all actions or decisions concerning children. In this regard, the EC and Member States will work to guarantee that all children have timely access to healthcare (including preventive care) and psychosocial support, as well as to formal education, regardless of the status of the child and/or of his/her parents (22).

[24] https://ec.europa.eu/health/health-eu-newsletter-202-focus_en#fragment2

4. National level

Migrant Integration Policy Index (MIPEX)

In collaboration with COST Action IS1103, Adapting European Health Systems to Diversity (ADAPT), and the Migration Policy Group (MPG), and within the Equi-Health project, IOM developed the Health strand of the MIPEX, an instrument for measuring the equitability of a country's policies. The MIPEX Health scores are based on the situation at the beginning of 2015.

a) Entitlements

The most fundamental element of accessing health services is entitlement to use the health system. It is linked first and foremost to the affordability of care and in practice, this usually means entitlement to participate in the scheme of health care coverage. Most European countries have either a tax-based or a statutory insurance-based system of coverage for health expenses, or a mixture of both (23). However, not everyone is entitled to join these systems, and entitlements for migrants vary from country to country (24) and according to the status of migrants.

Regular migrants are included, without any restrictions, in the national health systems and covered for the same basket of services as nationals in only 8 EU Member States (Belgium, Denmark, France, Germany, Italy, Luxembourg, Netherlands and Sweden). Conditional inclusion is granted in other Member States. If the conditions are satisfied, the same services are covered as for nationals. If not, regular migrants must pay health costs (other than for emergency care) out of pocket or through volunteer private insurances (23).

Besides legal entitlements, some administrative barriers can further hindered migrants' access to health services, in particular administrative demands from documents that may be difficult for migrants to produce and subjecting entitlements to discretionary decisions.

Only six EU Member States grant asylum seekers unconditional entitlement to the same range of services as nationals (France, Italy, Luxembourg, Netherlands, Spain and UK), while other countries impose two kinds of limitations. First, some treatments may be omitted from the standard package of services available; then, asylum seekers may, under certain conditions, be granted even less coverage. In addition, in 22 EU Member

States, asylum seekers can face administrative barriers that prevent them from enjoying the entitlements that the law provides.

The situation for migrants in an irregular situation (MIS) is dire. Many countries limit entitlements in the hope of encouraging MIS to leave the country and deterring others from coming. Four countries provide the same basket of service as nationals (Belgium, France, Luxembourg and the Netherlands) under some conditions. Three countries (Italy, Romania and Sweden) provide less health services that for nationals but more than emergency care without condition, while four countries (Denmark, Spain, Ireland and Malta) provide such extend of coverage but under certain conditions. Eight countries only provide emergency care but without pre-conditions (Austria, Estonia, Finland, Greece, Germany, Lithuania, Slovenia and Slovakia, while six countries provide emergency under certain conditions. Four EU Member States does not even cover emergency care (Bulgaria, Czech Republic, Latvia and Poland). Conditions include: inability to pay own medical bills, joining a social health insurance and paying premiums (Luxembourg), being a resident for more than three months (France and Portugal) or paying ten euros per consultation (Cyprus). In addition, administrative barriers are more frequent for MIS that for other migrants. To access services, documents difficult for migrants to obtain may be required and the concept of 'emergency' leads to administrative discretion, which may concern the decision as to whether care is sufficiently 'urgent' or 'essential', as well as whether the migrant can afford to pay for care themselves (either in cash or using private health insurance) (23).

b) Accessibility

Accessibility refers to the ability of people to actually utilise health facilities, goods and services, including through ensuring non-discrimination. The provision of equitable health services involves making sure that access to services and their quality do not differ between groups. "Equity of access" is determined not only by the entitlement to use the health system, but also by the availability of information for all about health and the health system; by making health services easily reachable and by minimising language and cultural barriers (24) .

Service providers appear to be badly informed about migrants' entitlements to health care. 11 EU member states (Bulgaria, Denmark, Germany,

Ireland, Latvia, Lithuania, Luxembourg, Malta, Poland, Slovakia and Slovenia) have no policy regarding the provision of information to health facilities and their employees about migrants' entitlements.

Regarding the provision of information about entitlements and use of health services to migrants, all EU Member States, except Hungary, are providing such information in languages other than the official languages of the country or English (except in the Netherlands).

Health education and promotion are less often provided. The lack of health promotion targeting migrants is particularly noticeable in Czech Republic, Greece, Croatia, Hungary, Luxembourg and Slovenia (23).

One of the problems undermining both the accessibility of health services for migrants and the quality of services is the existence of language barriers. Policies for provision of qualified interpreters free of charge to patients exist in only 12 EU Member States (i.e. Austria, Belgium, Denmark, Finland, Germany, Ireland, Italy, Luxembourg, Portugal, Spain and Sweden and the UK). Cultural mediation seems to be used in less than half of the EU Member States (23).

To be adapted to migrant's needs, health services also need to be "culturally competent" or "diversity-sensitive". Health services should take account of individual and family characteristics, experiences and situation, respect for different beliefs, religion, culture, competence in intercultural communication. In 13 EU countries there are standards or guidelines on culturally competent services, but these standards are not monitored by a relevant authority. Moreover, the MIPEX health strand highlights the lack of trainings and education for health service staff. In some countries policies exist to support training of staff in providing services responsive to the needs of migrants, in some others training may be part of basic professional education and or in service professional development.

Practice

Assessments performed by IOM between 2013 and 2016 in EU Member States, showed on one hand: insufficient health assessments in some countries, inadequate data collection and ineffective referral mechanisms for arriving migrants. In addition, administrative barriers, insufficient information sharing, lack of interpreters/mediators, health services not "culturally-competent" and lack of training further hinder the access to care for migrants.

Health assessment, data collection and referral mechanisms

a) Health assessment and screening upon arrival

As part of the Equi-Health "Fostering health provision for migrants, the Roma, and other vulnerable groups" project[25], co-financed by the EC's Directorate General for Health and Food Safety (DG SANTE), IOM conducted assessments of migrant, occupational and public health at EU's Southern Borders (Bulgaria, Croatia, Greece, Italy, Malta and Spain), based on desk review and field visits conducted between September 2013 and April 2014. In addition, during the spring 2016, IOM conducted the Scoping Study "Infectious disease health services for refugees and asylum seekers in Europe" for the European Centre for Disease Control (ECDC). The study consists of semi-structured interview of first line health professionals and representatives of national health authorities in two countries of first arrival (Greece and Italy), two countries of transit (Croatia and Slovenia) and two countries of destination (Austria and Sweden).

In Greece, in November 2013, there was no systematic screening for arriving migrants (25). A law (2745-29/10/2013) specified a common procedure for medical screening, psychosocial diagnosis and referral to be followed in first reception centers, but its implementation was seriously lacking. It was also reported that systematic screening was further obstructed by the lack of cooperation between public health and law enforcement authorities and the unclear distribution of responsibilities (26).

In Croatia, the assessment in April 2014 indicated that the lack of medical staff at the borders and in facilities was impeding the medical screening of migrants. However, all respondents interviewed as part of the Scoping Studies in May-June 2016, reported the presence of standardized procedures: all migrants undergo a medical examination after being placed in quarantine in reception centres, and are referred for specialised care if needed (26).

In Italy, the field visit in September 2013 evidenced some regular screening practices: medical first aid and screening at official points of entry was provided by Local Health Authorities, NGOs, and the Office of Maritime and Border Health under the Ministry of Health (26).

[25] For more information, see: http://equi-health.eea.iom.int/

Similarly in Malta, Austria and Sweden, at the time of the assessments, screening at arrival was regularly performed. In Malta, initial screening was done at disembarkation for emergency cases, dermatological or infectious disease and migrants were further screened for active tuberculosis and vaccinated in the centres. In Austria, a guideline issued by the Minister of Internal Affairs required a medical check-up within 24 hours of arrival (26). In Sweden, all asylum seekers were offered health assessment which in case of need could be followed by a referral to specialised care (27).

Data collection and referral mechanisms

Assessments in different countries indicate that health information is usually recorded but rarely shared. Each entity involved in the reception process uses their own procedures and templates, making the sharing of information between institutions difficult (26). The Scoping Study further indicates that a great variety of approaches exist in methods of registering data regarding health interventions conducted during the reception process, both between and within countries. Most systems, however, involve paper-based records and institution-specific templates. Respondents from Greece, Italy, Slovenia and Sweden reported that most of the time, health documents are given to migrants and that migrants might then bring them to other facilities they are transferred to. However, health professionals reported rarely receiving medical information when migrants are transferred under their area of responsibility (27).

Toward a Universal EU tool for migrant health assessments and continuity of care

To respond to the needs to harmonize health assessment practices, to improve data collection and to establish more efficient referral mechanism at local, national and EU level, a Handbook for Health Professionals was developed by the Migration Health Division of IOM. The handbook provides guidance on the health assessment process for migrants and refugees.[26] Based on this, the Personal Health Record (PHR) was produced with support from the EC and contribution from ECDC. The PHR helps to construct/reconstruct the medical history of arriving migrants, thereby

[26] More information at: http://re-health.eea.iom.int/electronic-health-database-project

establishing their health status and medical needs. It provides an opportunity to record subsequent provision of treatment, including vaccinations, and to offer counselling and health education services (28). Within the IOM/EC direct agreement Re-Health[27], IOM developed an electronic version of the PHR (e-PHR) and a platform to facilitate data entry, analysis and transfer within and between Member States. The e-PHR was piloted in Greece, Italy, Slovenia and Croatia and is further extended to Cyprus, Romania and Serbia within Re-Health2.

The implementation of the tool fosters a more holistic approach to migrants' health and improves the cooperation and coordination between reception centers and health services.

Provision of appropriate health services

Field assessments

In terms of provision of health services, main problems cited are insufficient human resources, especially in case of mass arrival, and the lack of trained interpreters/health mediators.

In Italy, assessments conducted in November 2013 indicated a lack of health personnel and that mental health was inadequately addressed throughout the reception procedure. Health professionals interviewed underlined that the lack of trained cultural mediators not only leads to communication problems, but also to difficulties in diagnosis because of their inability to correctly read the signs, symptoms and perceptions of illnesses in foreign patients, especially concerning mental health (26). Nevertheless, health professionals interviewed in May-June 2016 pointed to a well-organized cultural mediation service, including on ships, in hotspots and in reception centres (27).

In Malta, it was pointed out that regulations were unclear and confusing for both migrants and service providers, thus limiting migrants' access to services they are entitled to. Other obstacles include difficulties with

[27] The Re-Health project, co-funded under the amended EU Third Health Programme (2014-2020) by direct grant agreement awarded to IOM, was launched in February 2016. This project aims to ensure continuity of health care provision, limit the duplication of efforts and respective financial implications of repeated medical interventions (e.g. vaccinations, X–ray, etc.) and optimize the efforts in provision of proper health services at national and EU level.

transportation, lack of trust in doctors, perceived discriminatory practices, as well as a serious shortage of interpreters and cultural mediators (26).

In Bulgaria, there was a chronic shortage in health personnel and social support staff, including interpreters and mediators (26).

In Greece, health professionals interviewed in November 2013 indicated that migrants are systematically referred to hospitals although they could be more efficiently and economically treated by primary healthcare providers. Unfortunately, primary care services are not available for migrants, with the exception of some NGOs. The lack of interpreters and health mediators further limits migrants' access to health care (26). In 2016, Greek respondents indicated the availability of interpreters, but their number was insufficient to cover all languages and to respond to the high demand, especially in cases of mass entries (27).

In Sweden and in Croatia respondents indicated that interpreters were available in person or by telephone, or that informal interpreters belonging to the migrant's community were used, raising serious concerns regarding the accuracy of the interpretation and the privacy, with spill over effects on the quality and effectiveness of the health assistance provided. In addition, in both countries brochures, leaflets and pictures are also used (27).

Among countries assessed, only Slovenia and Austria report the availability of interpreters in nearly all cases/centres for the majority of languages (27).

Capacity building for health professionals (HPs) and law enforcement officers (LEOs)

IOM has a longstanding experience providing training on migration health. Within the "Increasing Public Health Safety along the New Eastern European Border Line – PHBLM" project (2007-2010), co-funded by the EC's DG SANTE, training material HPs and LEOs was developed and piloted in Hungary, Poland, Slovakia and Romania (29).

Within the above mentioned Equi-Health project and based on the needs identified, 2369 HPs and LEOs were trained during four training of trainers, 37 training sessions and one online training in Croatia, Germany, Greece, Italy, Malta, Portugal and Turkey. Topics included: communication and mass media, communicable and non-communicable diseases, first aid, mental health and psychosocial support, intercultural competences.

In addition, within the Re-Health project, 50 health mediators were trained in Croatia, Greece, Italy and Slovenia. Within the Re-Health[2], training of health mediators will be extended in Cyprus, Greece and Serbia.

5. Recommendations

Monitoring migrants' health

- Develop platforms for research, innovation and sharing of good practices at global and regional level (11).
- Promote the creation/ use of a common electronic platform for sharing data within and among countries to be used for individual care and for epidemiologic purposes (27)[28].

Policy and Legal Framework

- Establish, reinforce and monitor comprehensive national migrant health policies that are: rights-based, multi-sectoral and coordinated across sectors, participatory for migrants, civil society, private sector, and other key actors, based on the extension of Universal Health Coverage (UHC) and Social Protection to all migrants, irrespective of their migratory status (11)[29, 30].
- Focus equally on capacity to provide life-saving rapid interventions to migrants in need, as well as long-term strategies to mainstream migrant health within health and other sector strategies (11).

Migrant sensitive health system

- The principle of universal and equitable health coverage should be applied to all persons residing de facto in a country, regardless of their legal status (30).

[28] As mentioned above, the Electronic Personal Health Record (E-PHR) developed by IOM responds to this need. The electronic platform allows harmonizing health assessment practices within the EU and, at the same time, collecting data.
[29] In 2016, IOM in collaboration with COST ADAPT, published the "Recommendations on access to health services for migrants in an irregular situation: an expert consensus". The study, after presenting the framework of the existing EU policies wants to present clearly the arguments for improving access to health services for all(IOM, 2016).
[30] The Health Strand of the MIPEX, the instrument developed by IOM for measuring the equitability of a country's policies, responds to this need.

- Ensure the creation of adequate health and social support systems, including interpretation, cultural mediation, psychosocial assistance and staff training throughout the reception process (25).[31]
- Special attention must be paid to protecting the health-related rights of particularly vulnerable groups such as children, pregnant women and trafficked persons, regardless of whether such persons are residing regularly in the country (30)

Partnerships, network and multi-country framework

- Enhance political leadership, partnership, and mobilization of resources towards innovation, participation and action to respond to health needs and challenges brought by global migration (11).
- Enhance cross-border cooperation, partnerships and communication between institutions and levels (EH summary) to harmonize policies and practices and ensure continuity of care and health responses to emerging needs linked to human mobility, including in health and border management (11)[32].
- Ensure the mainstreaming of migration health issues within regional and multi-regional dialogues on health, migration, development, international cooperation and enhance cooperation among countries (11).
- Ensure a dedicated space for health within the Global Compact on Migration (11).
- Promote the migration health agenda across-sectors and within the scope of the implementation of the SDGs (11).

[31] Researches and field assessments show an overall low level or lack of knowledge on migrant and refugee-related health problems among personnel working with these groups. Supporting EU Member States in reducing knowledge gaps of different categories of health professionals, law enforcement officers and other security bodies in respect to health-related border policies and health challenges faced by migrant populations is an important objective of EU Health policies. In this framework, IOM in collaboration with GIZ and the London School of Tropical medicine is developing a training programme to reinforce the skills of professionals working with migrants and refugees, at first point of arrival, transit and destination countries.

[32] As highlighted in the research carried out by IOM between 2013 and 2015 at EU' southern borders, the need to develop shared/horizontal protocols common to all actors involved in the reception process, to identify and assign tasks, and provide coordinated and standardized services throughout the reception process is crucial.

References

(1) International Organization for Migration. Global Migration Trends Factsheet 2015 [Internet]. Berlin: International Organization for Migration; 2016 p. 1-19. Available from: https://publications.iom.int/system/files/global_migration_trends_2015_factsheet.pdf

(2) United Nations Development Programme. Human Development Report 2009 - Overcoming barriers: Human mobility and development [Internet]. New York: United Nations Development Programme; 2009 p. 1-217. Available from: http://hdr.undp.org/sites/default/files/reports/269/hdr_2009_en_complete.pdf

(3) de la Rica S, Glitz A, Ortega F. Immigration in Europe: Trends, Policies and Empirical Evidence [Internet]. Bonn: Institute for the Study of Labor (IZA); 2013. Available from: http://ftp.iza.org/dp7778.pdf

(4) International Organization for Migration. Mixed Migration Flows in the Mediterranean and Beyond - Compilation of available data and information - 2015 [Internet]. 2015 p. 1-21. Available from: https://www.iom.int/sites/default/files/situation_reports/file/Mixed-Flows-Mediterranean-and-Beyond-Compilation-Overview-2015.pdf

(5) United Nations. UN Summit for Refugees and Migrants 2016 [Internet]. Refugees and Migrants. Available from: http://refugeesmigrants.un.org/summit

(6) World Health Organization. Health of migrants: the way forward - report of a global consultation, Madrid, Spain, 3-5 March 2010 [Internet]. Geneva: World Health Organization; 2010 p. 1-112. Available from: https://health.iom.int/sites/default/files/Health-of-Migrants.pdf

(7) World Health Organization. Health of migrants [Internet]. 2008 p. 1-3. Available from: http://apps.who.int/iris/bitstream/10665/23533/1/A61_R17-en.pdf

(8) International Organization for Migration. Healthy Migrants in Healthy Communities: promoting and delivering quality health care for migrants and host communities [Internet]. Geneva: International Organization for Migration; 2017 p. 1-4. Available from: https://www.iom.int/sites/default/files/our_work/DMM/Migration-Health/MHD_Factsheet_General_EN.pdf

(9) Goal 10 targets [Internet]. United Nations Development Programme. Available from: http://www.undp.org/content/undp/en/home/sustainable-development-goals/goal-10-reduced-inequalities/targets/

(10) United Nations. Leaving no one behind [Internet]. The Sustainable Development Goals Report 2016. 2018. Available from: https://unstats.un.org/sdgs/report/2016/leaving-no-one-behind

(11) International Organization for Migration. The Health of Migrants: A core cross-cutting theme [Internet]. 2017 p. 1-9. Available from: https://www.iom.

int/sites/default/files/our_work/ODG/GCM/IOM-Thematic-Paper-Health-of-Migrants.pdf
(12) United Nations. International Migration Report - 2015 [Internet]. New York: United Nations; 2016 p. 1-27. Available from: http://www.un.org/en/development/desa/population/migration/publications/migrationreport/docs/MigrationReport2015.pdf
(13) World Health Organization. Promoting the health of refugees and migrants [Internet]. 2017 p. 1. Available from: http://apps.who.int/gb/ebwha/pdf_files/EB140/B140(9)-en.pdf
(14) 2nd Global Consultation on Migrant Health: Resetting the Agenda [Internet]. International Organization for Migration. 2017. Available from: https://www.iom.int/migration-health/second-global-consultation
(15) International Organization for Migration. Colombo Statement [Internet]. 2017 p. 1-3. Available from: https://www.iom.int/sites/default/files/our_work/DMM/Migration-Health/colombo_statement.pdf
(16) European Commission. A Common European Asylum System [Internet]. Luxembourg: European Union; 2014 p. 1-9. Available from: https://ec.europa.eu/home-affairs/sites/homeaffairs/files/e-library/docs/ceas-fact-sheets/ceas_factsheet_en.pdf
(17) The Council of the European Union. Council Directive 2003/9/EC of 27 January 2003 laying down minimum standards for the reception of asylum seekers [Internet]. 2003 p. 1-8. Available from: http://eur-lex.europa.eu/LexUriServ/LexUriServ.do?uri=OJ:L:2003:031:0018:0025:En:PDF
(18) Peiro M, Petrova-Benedict R. Migrant health policy. The Portuguese and Spanish EU Presidencies. Eurohealth-Migration and Health in the European Union. 2010;16(1):1-4.
(19) European Parliament resolution of 8 March 2011 on reducing health inequalities in the EU (2010/2089(INI)) [Internet]. European Parliament. 2011. Available from: http://www.europarl.europa.eu/sides/getDoc.do?pubRef=-//EP//TEXT+TA+P7-TA-2011-0081+0+DOC+XML+V0//EN
(20) European Commision. Action Plan on the integration of third country nationals - Communication from the Commission to the European Parliament, the Council, the European Economic and Social Committee and the Committee of the Regions. [Internet]. Brussels: European Commission; 2016 p. 1-21. Available from: https://ec.europa.eu/home-affairs/sites/homeaffairs/files/what-we-do/policies/european-agenda-migration/proposal-implementation-package/docs/20160607/communication_action_plan_integration_third-country_nationals_en.pdf
(21) Establishing a European Pillar of Social Rights - Communication from the Commission to the European Parliament, the Council, the European

Economic and Social Committee of the Regions [Internet]. EUR-Lex Access to European Union law. 2017. Available from: http://eur-lex.europa.eu/legal-content/EN/ALL/?uri=COM:2017:0250:FIN

(22) European Commission. Communication from the Commission to the European Parliament and the Council. The protection of children in migration [Internet]. Brussels: European Commission; 2017 p. 1-17. Available from: https://ec.europa.eu/home-affairs/sites/homeaffairs/files/what-we-do/policies/european-agenda-migration/20170412_communication_on_the_protection_of_children_in_migration_en.pdf

(23) International Organization for Migration. Summary Report on the MIPEX Health Strand and Country Reports [Internet]. Geneva: International Organization for Migration; 2016 p. 1-124. Available from: https://publications.iom.int/system/files/mrs_52.pdf

(24) Rechel B, Mladovsky P, Devillé W, Rijks B, Petrova-Benedict R, McKee M. Migration and health in the European Union. Maidenhead, England: McGraw Hill/Open University Press; 2011.

(25) International Organization for Migration. Equi-Health, Report on the mechanism of data collection [Internet]. 2015 p. 1-81. Available from: http://equi-health.eea.iom.int/images/Data_collection_report.pdf

(26) International Organization for Migration. Assessment Report: Health Situation at EU's Southern Borders - Migrant, Occupational, and Public Health. 2015.

(27) International Organization for Migration / European Centre for Disease Prevention and Control. Scoping Study "Infectious Disease health services for refugees and asylum seekers in Europe" (unpublished). 2016.

(28) European Parliament. The public health dimension of the European migrant crisis [Internet]. 2016 p. 1-8. Available from: http://www.europarl.europa.eu/RegData/etudes/BRIE/2016/573908/EPRS_BRI(2016)573908_EN.pdf

(29) International Organization for Migration. Increasing Public Health Safety alongside the New Eastern European Border Line [Internet]. Brussels: International Organization for Migration; p. 1-3. Available from: https://www.iom.int/jahia/webdav/shared/shared/mainsite/activities/health/PHBLM-Project-Summary-Brief-011209.pdf

(30) International Organization for Migration. Equi-Health, Recommendations on access to health services for migrants in an irregular situation: an expert consensus [Internet]. Brussels: International Organization for Migration; 2016 p. 1-59. Available from: http://equi-health.eea.iom.int/images/Expert_consensus_Recommendations.pdf

CHAPTER 4

Migration and Health Policies: considerations on the Portuguese context

PEDRO CALADO
High Commissioner for Migration, Portugal

CRISTINA CASAS
Coordinator of the Migration Policy Unit
High Commission for Migration, Portugal

1. Introduction

The High Commission for Migration (ACM) has been responsible for immigrant integration policies, now extended to include refugees and asylum seekers. As such, ACM has actively collaborated in three major areas: i) definition, execution and evaluation of public policies related to migration; ii) integration of migrants and ethnic groups and iii) management and valuing of diversity.

ACM is integrated in the Presidency of the Council of Ministers and due to the transversal nature of its mandate (touching upon various areas of intervention), a large part of the work developed in the area of integration and diversity management has been in close articulation with the different relevant sectorial public entities and through partnerships with civil society entities, giving special focus to the Immigrant Associations and Non-Governmental Organizations.

As such, striving for holistic and effective integration public policies have been conceived, developed and implemented. Varied initiatives, projects and activities have been conducted, which have become indispensable answers to the issues that arise with migration; some of which have been recognized – nationally and internationally – as good practices.

Some examples of these good practices include the opening of two National Support Centres for the Integration of Migrants (CNAIM) in 2004, in Lisbon and in Porto, and the opening in 2009 of the Faro CNAIM. Following the One-Stop-Shop model, it was possible to gather and ensure cooperation, under the same space and identical working philosophy, all public institutions related to immigration. This allows immigrants to be able to resolve different issues related to their integration process in Portugal in the same location and with one visit.

In parallel, understanding the dispersion of immigrant communities throughout the Portuguese territory and the local institutions' interest in the development of answers targeting these communities, Local Support Centers for the Integration of Migrants (CLAIM) were created. The CLAIM aim to promote integration based on proximity and decentralized, resulting from partnerships between ACM and municipalities or civil society organizations, in close articulation with the CNAIM.

More recently, in 2016, following an integrated services logic, an adaptation of the national and local structures was conducted through Ordinance 203/2016, from 25 July, creating the National Support Network for the Integration of Migrants (RNAIM). This Network was readjusted to respond to the new migration realities and challenges, namely in regard to the integration of refugee people.

In the last decades, Portugal, as many other countries in the world, witnessed high growth in the number of immigrants; from a country of emigration, it became a country of immigration. Until 1980, immigration had never surpassed 50,000 residents. Between 1986 and 1997 the number of foreigners doubled, going from 87,000 to 175,000. In the decade between 1990 and 2000, immigration to Portugal doubled, and again doubled only two years later (2000 to 2002) to reach 400,000 immigrants, representing 4% of the Portuguese population and 8% of the active population (Oliveira e Gomes, 2014).

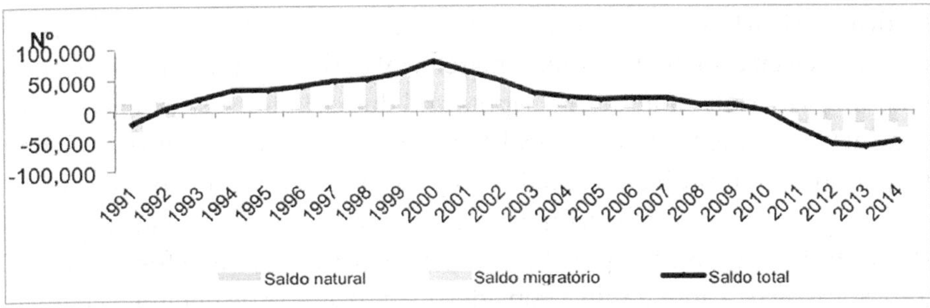

Source: INE – Live-birth Statistics, deaths and Annual Population Estimates.

Early on, the perception that Portugal had become a country of immigration gave space for concern with the integration of these populations. This new reality incited various types of difficulties, not only to the Portuguese State that was not prepared for this flow, but also to civil society organizations.

Overview of interventions of some projects

The need for urgent intervention to minimize injustice and protect vulnerable migrant groups was at the centre of ACMs mandate. Indeed, the intention to create humane structures that provide resolution to problems and/or obstacles, build respect for the different nationalities, cultures, religions and, above all, the dignity of the human being, was the motivation for ACM's creation of the National Support Centres for the Integration of Migrants.

Following the principles in which the CNAIM were founded – working in cooperation, under the same roof and with the same working philosophy – and among other services, the Health Office was created in partnership with the Ministry of Health. The Health Office has been open for over 10 years and gives health information and support, also providing important mediation and articulation work with other services. Between the start date and 30 September 2017, 10,077 services have been provided to migrants.

This Office provides telephone and in-person consultations regarding health services; identifies eventual problems in migrants' access to the National Health Service, aiming at a speedy resolution; articulates with health institutions, community structures and the different Offices in CNAIM, evaluation of symptoms and referral to the adequate services; provides information on migrants' rights and duties in access to health care; conducts training targeted to health professionals and migrants; collaborates in research projects related to migration and health, among others.

The possibility of delivering information by telephone to immigrants through the Migrant Support Hotline, dispensing the need for a physical journey, is also of added value, considering it can provide general clarifications regarding immigration to immigrant citizens and their associations, employers, public administration bodies and other interested citizens.

The Telephone Translation Service, that places simultaneously through a telephone conversation the institution/service professional, the translator and the immigrant, in order to overcome linguistic barriers, is a resource that has been widely used within and outside of ACM's services.

Using a network of 56 translators/interpreters that master one or more languages in addition to Portuguese, diverse institutions such as municipalities, conservatories, hospitals, health centres, schools, courts and other public and private organisms involved in the welcoming and integration of immigrants have relied on this service.

Health and migrants

Studies have shown that, on arrival, migrants show, on average, better health indicators than the resident population (Dias, 2007, 2017; Oliveira e Gomes, 2017) The main reasons are linked to the natural selection process resulting from the migratory cycle. In addition, if it's true that in the countries of origin many migrants have contact with some pathologies, the same identic phenomenon happens in relation to other pathologies in the host country. Recent studies regarding refugees who arrived in Europe support that evidence. Also, some have arguing that exposure to risks is greater in the host countries than in the countries of origin. Some explanations derive from difficult socioeconomic conditions associated to the hardship of life of immigrants deficient housing conditions; working in dangerous professions; and fear of contact with the health system (Oliveira e Pires, 2010).

However, it is important to underline that when socioeconomic deprivation occurs it affects health conditions of the migrant population as well as those of the resident population. Health status tends to depend on the socioeconomic context, and several illnesses are associated to poverty and social exclusion.

Some associated to mental health, susceptible to depression, are aggravated by solitude, integration difficulties, missing family and friends or by experiencing discrimination episodes in the host countries.

There are some specificities associated to mental health in that susceptibility to depression among others are aggravated by solitude, integration difficulties, missing family and friends or by experiencing discrimination episodes in host countries (Viana, 2010)

Key concerns in the health area

An attempt was made to provide responses to several constraints through the creation of structures and services for global integration; however, some constraints with direct impact on migrant health persist. Some of these constraints include: difficult social conditions (in regard to housing conditions and social environment); cultural factors (experienced by migrants and also health professionals); language barriers that often hinder an effective communication between health professionals and migrants; insufficient adaption of existing services to the new migration profiles (namely refugees); lack of information among migrants of existing services and how to access them; some lack of knowledge by migrants of their rights and duties and access conditions to the National Health Service; low health literacy, among others.

To respond to some of these difficulties and concerns, legislation was published and important political instruments were created in order to counteract the obstacles and create new mechanisms to answer the needs of the migrant community.

2. Specific Legislation

Another fundamental aspect to highlight was the publication of legislation in order to establish access conditions for immigrants (even in irregular situation) to the National Health Service.

Some important legislation includes Order nº. 25 360/2001, from 16 November 2001, followed by the information circular nº. 12/DQS/DMD, from 7 May 2009 issued by the General Directorate for Health

(DGS), which clarified some aspects related to the application of the 2001 Order.

In addition, Law nº 67/2004 from March created a national registry to guarantee access of minors to health care and preschool and school regardless of their legal situation in Portugal.

3. Public Policy Instruments

The National Plans for Immigrant Integration (PII I and II) – 2007-2010 and 2010-2013 – are political instruments of great relevance, with one dedicated area focused on health intervention. The National Plans used different measures and goals for which in its pursuit involving diverse public entities, with particular relevance for the General Directorate of Health, the Regional Health Administration and the High Commission for Migration.

The measures included improving aspects such as the promotion of migrants' access to the National Health Service, intercultural training for health professionals, developing partnerships between public services and of those with civil society, and improving and clarification of procedures in health agreements, among others.

As an example, one of the measures involved the creation and implementation of a reception manual for access by foreign citizens to the health system; this was published by Directorate-General of Health as a result of the second Integration of Immigrants Plan (measure 39) that aimed to clarify and harmonize different procedures in the National Health System.

The Strategic Plan for Migration (PEM), approved by Council of Ministers Resolution nº 12-B/2015 from 20 March 2015, in place until 2020, adopts a wider perspective and gives continuity, including further detail of work themes, with the implementation of measures considered essential in the health area.

The 106 measures are distributed through the 5 priority political Axis of the immigrant integration policies: the policies to promote the integration of new nationals, coordination policies of migration flows, policies strengthening the migratory legality and quality of migration services, and polices to foster the monitoring and support of the return of national emigrant citizens. The health measures are integrated in the first axis – immigrant integration policies.

Some of the areas foreseen in these measures include:

- *increasing monitoring of health in vulnerable populations, namely immigrants,* through the elaboration of studies;
- *clarification of the normative framework application in regards to immigrants' access, in irregularity situation, to the National Health Service* and of the *implementation and monitoring of the Reception Manual of Foreign Citizens in the Health System*;
- *creation of accessible information about the health system* - dissemination of information regarding rights and duties and the way in which the National Health Service works;
- *promotion of training for health professionals on the needs of migrants in the health area* – measures that follow a logic of continuous improvement and adaptation. (ACM, 2015)

Following the same logic, ACM is also involved in the execution of Sectorial Plans, coordinated by other Ministries, such as the National Health Plan, the National Strategy Against Female Genital Mutilation, among others, where the specificities of migrant communities are contemplated.

The importance of health for all citizens in general forces us to be particularly aware of obstacles that might arise for migrants and refugees. The Council for Migration is a consultative body to support and participate in the definition of ACM's lines of conduct, assuring the participation and collaboration of public and private entities in the definition and execution of migration policy. It is an important instrument which, by involving representatives of the main communities living in Portugal and institutions more directly related to migration policy, can effectively put in place, monitor and implement public polices in diverse domains, such as in health.

4. Future perspectives

Investment in aspects such as health literacy, education, promotion of health and health professionals' training should continue, taking into consideration issues of social, culture and linguistics levels, that often arise in relation to these populations.

New tendencies, realities and fragilities demand a permanent and close "watch" by all – including politicians, those responsible for the institutions, health professionals and technicians, migrants, patients and society in general – in order to find gains and quality in health policies.

By working together in a coordinated manner, efforts to maintain and deepen this process to achieve greater gains in health continues. This collaborative process has been a source national and international pride, for health improvements and in the construction of a more inclusive and humane Portugal (ACM, 2010, 2015).

Further work is being developed in areas such as the future launch of applications for the "Municipal and Intercultural Mediators Project," financed by POISE (European Social Fund – Operational Programme Social Inclusion and Employment); here mediators will intervene in various areas, namely health, to support health professionals, facilitate communication between local communities and public services, create networks in the health area and work in the prevention and management of conflicts.

The implementation of the measures foreseen in the Strategic Plan for Migration, particularly those related to health will continue, with support and partnerships between the High Commission for Migration and the Ministry of Health/General Directorate for Health.

It is important to highlight the launch of the project "Promotion of integration through Health Equity" in 2017, which resulted from a partnership between the International Organization for Migration (IOM), the Directorate General for Health, the ISCTE - University Institute of Lisbon (ISCTE-IUL) and the five Regional Health Administrations, co-financed by ACM while designated under authority of the Asylum, Migration and Integration Fund (AMIF). In addition to offering training for health care providers, this project also included transfer of the tool "Equity Standards in Health Care" to Portugal, developed by the *Task Force Migrant-Friendly and Culturally Competent Health and Care*, aimed at providing a *"guided auto evaluation"* in health services.

The investment in the dissemination of the training offer, free of charge and in short duration modules targeting citizens, professionals and entities that, directly or indirectly are linked to Interculturality and Migration issues, is also a priority. These materials are based on the promotion of a positive and enriching cultural diversity management, through intercultural and interreligious dialogue, based on the respect for the Constitution and the law, valuing cultural diversity in a framework of development and mutual respect. Their objectives involve, among others, the promotion of a better understanding of cultural diversity, raising awareness for welcoming and integrating immigrants in Portugal; and providing training on interculturality. As such this training offer has diverse themes, namely those related to intercultural dialogue and interculturality and migrants' access to health. In order to make the health service network and its functioning regulations and procedures understandable by the different migrants, the High Commission for Migration has worked together with the General Directorate of Health in simplifying and translating materials in various languages.

In complement, wide dissemination of all information to migrants, in order that all useful information reaches the widest number of people, is made through the High Commission for Migration's Network of partners and services, such as the National and Local Support Centres for the Integration of Migrants, Immigrant Associations and the Choices Programme.

Investing in new Municipal Plans for the Integration of Immigrants, presently 19, which include health measures, is a big asset to work collaboratively at the local level.

Conclusion

The integration of migrants, namely in the health domain, is ongoing. We believe however, that in Portugal, the frankly generous legal framework on access to health (namely when compared to other contexts) has come to contribute to guarantee equity, assuring that all migrants regardless of their national, ethnic or religious origin find services truly opened to diversity, including in the health sector.

ACM has been investing in the design of an intercultural society, and increasingly in the domain of health. This is a challenge requiring continued attention, but mostly actions, from the whole government but also whole society, to guarantee the safeguard of a fundamental right.

References

(1) ACM, I. P. II Plan for Immigrant Integration (2010-2013). Lisbon: ACM, I.P. Publishing; 2010. Available from (English version): http://www.acm.gov.pt/documents/10181/222357/PII_2010_2013_ing.pdf/2de54891-737b-4263-ba2c-16fb8538ba60.

(2) ACM. I. P. Strategic Plan for Migration (2015-2020). Lisbon: ACM, I.P. Publishing; 2015. Available from (English version): http://www.acm.gov.pt/documents/10181/222357/PEM_ACM_final.pdf/9ffb3799-7389-4820-83ba-6dcfe22c13fb.
(3) Dias, Sónia (org) (2007), Imigração e Saúde, *Revista Migrações,* Observatório da Imigração, Lisboa: ACIDI.
(4) Dias, S. (2017) (coord.), *Os migrantes são um risco para a população dos países de acolhimento?*(http://news.cision.com/pt/instituto-de-higiene-e-medicina-tropical/r/os-migrantes-sao-um-risco-para-apopulacao-dos-paises-de-acolhimento-,c636323521060000000).
(5) Oliveira C, Gomes N. (2014) Monitoring the Integration of Immigrants in Portugal: Decennial Statistical Report. Collection of Immigration in Numbers of the Migration Observatory. Lisbon: ACM, I.P. Publishing; 2014. Available from (Portuguese version): http://www.om.acm.gov.pt/documents/58428/179573/RelatorioDecenalImigracaoNumeros2014web.pdf/d4aaef2b-2e21-4475-9202-70a25433a81b.
(6) Oliveira C, Gomes N. (2017) Monitoring the Integration of Immigrants in Portugal: Annual Statistical Report. Collection of Immigration in Numbers of the Migration Observatory. Lisbon: ACM, I.P. Publishing; 2017. Available from (Portuguese version): http://www.om.acm.gov.pt/documents/58428/383402/Relat%C3%B3rio+Indicadores+de+Integra%C3%A7%C3%A3o+de+Imigrantes+OM+2017.pdf/432839ce-f3c2-404f-9b98-39ab22b5edc5.
(7) Oliveira C, Pires C. (2010) Immigration and Accident Rate. Collection of Studies of the Migration Observatory. Lisbon: ACM, I.P. Publishing; 2010. Available from (Portuguese version): http://www.om.acm.gov.pt/documents/58428/177157/OI_41.pdf/c172e1ab-223b-4079-b812-e1e9419abe8c.
(8) Viana, V. (2010) Saúde mental, qualidade de vida e acesso aos cuidados de saúde na comunidade brasileira de Lisboa. ACM, I. P. Publishing. Available from (Portuguese version): http://www.om.acm.gov.pt/documents/58428/179891/Tese31WEB.pdf/135444aa-f682-4e8b-accb-74e5f0fbc9e4.
(9) Burnett, Angela e Peel, Michael (2001), “Health needs of asylium Seekers and refugees”, in BMJ, volume 322, pp 544-547.

CHAPTER 5

Asylum Seekers and Refugees in Portugal: an overview

Teresa Tito de Morais
Board President of the Portuguese Council for Refugees (CPR), Portugal

Portugal has been a country which welcomed refugees and scored high in terms of protection, reception, as well as good cooperation among the central Government, local authorities and Non-governmental Organizations. Although Portugal receives a small number of asylum applications annually, it has seen a significant increase in recent years that impacted the national asylum system and caused overcrowding of reception facilities, as we will further analyse.

It is estimated by the Portuguese Immigration Service (SEF) that there were 1,500 refugees (550 recognized refugees and an additional 950 persons with subsidiary protection) living in Portugal at end year 2016[33] – a number that undoubtedly will change in the upcoming years.

Indeed, Portugal's role in the reception of asylum seekers and refugees has increased in the past few years, receiving not only persons arriving spontaneously at border points or national territory, but also persons arriving under solidarity mechanisms, such as relocation and resettlement.

[33] Number provided by the Asylum and Refugee Department of the Portuguese Immigration Service (SEF) that refers to foreign citizens entitled with valid documents.

If in 2007 Portugal received only 200 requests for international protection, by 2017 this number was 1.010[34], an increase of 405%, according to figure 1.

Figure 1. Spontaneous international protection applications filed in Portugal between 2007 and 2017

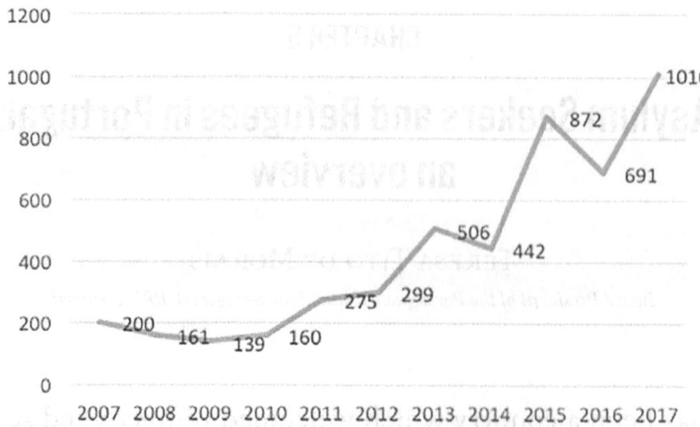

Added to these spontaneous requests are the national applicants from Syria, Iraq and Eritrea who arrived in Portugal under the referred Solidarity Programs, namely about 1532 persons[35] via the Relocation Program and about 142 via the Resettlement Program[36].

Briefly, relocation is the transfer of persons who are in need of or already benefit from a form of international protection in one EU Member State to another EU Member State where they would be granted similar protection. Eligibility for the relocation scheme is limited to applicants who are

[34] Provisional data from SEF for 2017.

[35] As of 12th March, 2018. More information in https://ec.europa.eu/home-affairs/sites/homeaffairs/files/what-we-do/policies/european-agenda-migration/press-material/docs/state_of_play_-_relocation_en.pdf

[36] Resettlement of Syrian refugees from Turkey after 4 April 2016. More information in https://ec.europa.eu/home-affairs/sites/homeaffairs/files/what-we-do/policies/european-agenda-migration/press-material/docs/state_of_play_-_eu-turkey_en.pdf

in clear need of international protection and are a national or stateless resident of those countries for which the EU-wide average recognition rate is more than 75 percent, namely beneficiaries from Syria, Eritrea and Iraq[37].

As for resettlement, it is the transfer of non-EU national or stateless persons who have been identified as in need of international protection to an EU state where they are admitted either on humanitarian grounds or with the status of refugee.

Challenges ahead lie with the successful implementation of the relocation and resettlement programs in Portugal, given that it will require efforts to address shortcomings related to reception, integration (including health issues, as described further ahead), coordination and capacity building amongst stakeholders, and maintenance of high standards of protection for this vulnerable population (namely legal assistance to all asylum seekers at all stages of procedure, monitoring the quality of asylum procedure and promoting alternatives to detention).

The current presentation begins with a description of what are the most common diseases among refugees and asylum seekers in Portugal, based on the experience of the Portuguese Refugee Council[38] (CPR). In a second part, it will be described the main challenges related to the access of this population to health.

Indisputably, one of the priorities of the CPR's work is refugee health, as it is for the United Nations High Commissioner for Refugees (UNHCR), which states that *"refugees must have access to health services*

[37] More information in http://eea.iom.int/index.php/what-we-do/eu-relocation

[38] Conselho Português para os Refugiados (CPR), founded in 1991, is the leading Development NGO in Portugal working on asylum and refugee issues. CPR's core activities include to play a consultative role in refugee status determination procedures and to provide free legal aid to asylum seekers and refugees at all stages of the asylum procedure. It is also mandated to provide initial reception and social support to asylum seekers, relocated and resettled refugees, as well as promoting their integration in the Portuguese society with assistance for employment and training, and Portuguese language classes.

CPR runs two reception centres for refugees in Portugal, one of them dedicated to the support of unaccompanied refugee minors. The inauguration of a third centre is scheduled for the end of 2018. CPR also seeks to raise public awareness and mainstream refugee rights into public debate for a more inclusive society notably through advocacy initiatives (conferences, seminars, training courses). CPR was awarded with the "Human Rights Award" of the Portuguese Parliament, in 2000.

available at similar costs or lower than those of nationals". In fact, this United Nations Agency mentions the *"experiences of displacement due to armed conflict, persecution or disaster place psychological and social stress on individuals, families and communities. The way refugees experience and respond to loss, pain, disruption and violence varies significantly and can, in many ways, affect their mental health and psychosocial well-being or increase their vulnerability to developing mental health problems*[39]*."*

The psychological and social problems of refugees are, as a rule, normal reactions to intense living conditions, specifically traumatic experiences, such as war, torture or detention, but also losses of close relatives and everything that is familiar, adversities during the fleeing process, the uncertainty arising from lengthy asylum procedures, possible changes in the family structure, inadequate parenting and much more. The problems are thus of a physical, psychological and social nature, and must be adequately answered.

The emotional stress caused by forced displacement has, precisely, a great impact on physical and mental health. Harassment, physical violence and suffering will, in many cases, be added to the trauma of displacement, and together they will drain the physical and emotional reserves of the refugees, causing the loss of their natural resistance to diseases.

Throughout more than 26 years of intervention with refugees, we have seen that the most frequent health problems of this population are injuries caused by firearms and explosives, such as those resulting from burns, a consequence of exposure to war contexts, cardiovascular problems and hypertension, in addition to issues related to mental health, thus corroborating many WHO studies[40].

Living conditions in overcrowded places, namely emergency refugee camps, facilitate the spread of infectious diseases, such as tuberculosis, thus affecting the lives of thousands of refugees. In addition, severe dermatological problems such as dermatitis and scabies, associated with poor

[39] UN High Commissioner for Refugees (UNHCR), *Operational Guidance: Mental Health & Psychosocial Support Programming for Refugee Operations*, 2013, available at: http://www.refworld.org/docid/53a3ebfb4.html [accessed 3 October 2017]

[40] More information in http://www.euro.who.int/en/health-topics/health-determinants/migration-and-health/migrant-health-in-the-european-region/migration-and-health-key-issues#292115

hygiene of these places where refugees are forced to live, leading to the development and spread of skin diseases[41].

Refugees report upon arrival significant problems related to oral health, with negative consequences on their quality of life. During prolonged toothaches, refugees describe difficulties related with food intake, hence compromising their nutrition. The difficulties are aggravated by the limited financial resources of refugees, which prevents them from accessing certain treatments on arrival in a host country.

Refugees also report joint problems (back / shoulder, knee pains), some caused by travels and by staying in confined spaces for extended periods. Refugee women can experience specific problems, especially related to complications associated with pregnancy and childbirth, the health of their new-borns and children, and other sexual and reproductive health problems[42]. In this regard, access to quality reproductive health services, including appropriate emergency obstetric care, can dramatically reduce the number of women dying during or after childbirth and ensure that mothers and children enjoy a healthy life. CPR is currently implementing an Age, Gender and Diversity (AGD) Strategy at the Refugee Centre, and a participatory assessment, hence recognizing that "all refugees are vulnerable, but age, gender, or other identities, and shortcomings should be understood as a cause of even greater vulnerability."[43]

As regards children, they tend to experience acute infectious diseases (mainly respiratory), episodes of diarrhoea and skin diseases which, as is the case of adults, are due to poor health and hygiene during migration.

In order to respond to these health-related challenges, CPR has established agreements with dental clinics, ophthalmic centres and medical analyses laboratories which provide free care to refugees.

[41] Wollina U, Gaber B, Mansour R, Langner D, Hansel G, Koch A. Dermatologic Challenges of Health Care for Displaced People. Lessons from a German Emergency Refugee Camp. Our Dermatol Online. 2016;7(2):136-138.

[42] For more information, please see UNHCR's global Strategy for Public Health (2014 – 2018);

[43] Fore more information "UN High Commissioner for Refugees (UNHCR), *UNHCR Age, Gender and Diversity - Accountability Report 2016*, June 2017, available at: http://www.refworld.org/docid/595cda5d4.html [accessed 3 October 2017]"

CPR also works closely with the São João da Talha local health centre, the Pulmonology Diagnosis Centre and the Public Health Delegation, which performs regular child and adult-targeted vaccination campaigns at the Refugee Reception Centre.

However, despite significant improvement in health service provision to refugees, we believe that a number of challenges require urgent response.

Main challenges in healthcare access by international protection applicants and beneficiaries

Under applicable law, international protection candidates and beneficiaries (both recognized refugees and beneficiaries of subsidiary protection), along with their family members, are entitled to access the Portuguese National Health Service (Serviço Nacional de Saúde – SNS). Specifically, this means that international protection applicants are *"entitled to free access to both emergency and primary healthcare, as well as drug treatment, which is to be provided by eligible health services in the relevant area of residence"*. Applicants are thus entitled to ambulatory general practice care, mother-child care, family planning, school planning and elderly care, as well as specialist care (i.e. ophthalmology, dental care, otolaryngology and mental health), hospital admission into non-differentiated car and nursing services, including house visitation[44].

As such, in Portugal, legal obstacles to healthcare access are, in practice, non-existent.

It is thus important to acknowledge improvement in healthcare access for refugees, particularly out-of-pocket payments exemption. Law 26/2014 enforces large-scope access to the Portuguese National Health Service. Further, Ordinance 24/2014[45] provides for the enlargement of rights enjoyed by international protection applicants and beneficiaries.

However, a number of administrative obstacles against the full enjoyment of rights, as established under law, persist. Obstacles may be split into two categories:

[44] More information in http://mobilidade.dgs.pt/cidadaosestrangeiros/Paginas/Acesso-sistema-sa%C3%BAde-cidad%C3%A3os-estrangeiros-estatuto-refugiado-ou-direito-de-asilo-em-Portugal.aspx

[45] Retrived from http://www2.acss.min-saude.pt/Portals/0/Circular%20Normativa%2024-2014.pdf

- On the one hand, National Health Service insufficiencies, which affects all beneficiaries, are particularly acute as regards international protection applicants and beneficiaries, who commonly suffer from health issues which require immediate post-arrival and constant support. Waiting for the allocation of a General Practitioner and operational problems in determining which exemptions are to be enjoyed by refugees are also real obstacles which hamper this population's clinical stabilization;
- On the other hand, CPR observes that access to drug treatments continues to be difficult, although legal norms enforce this. As a result, CPR often allocates a large part of its budget to the provision of drug treatment-related fees.

Furthermore, a technical and intercultural deficit in National Health Service institutions remains. There is a particular lack of expertise on the clinical needs of refugees in healthcare institutions which show low levels of experience in migrant support, namely in rural areas. Additionally, National Health Service workers show low levels of intercultural competences. This may stem from a lack of training on the specific needs of forced migrants.

Territorial asymmetries in healthcare provision are a clear problem with regard to refugee access to healthcare. Given the specific vulnerability profile apparent in this population, asymmetries in healthcare coverage result in disadvantages to refugees living in rural areas or health districts with specific needs (e.g. the Algarve region).

It is our perception that, if a refugee requires special care concerning common disease patterns stemming from forced displacement, being distant from hospitals or other healthcare facilities is not only an obstacle to care but is also an impediment and a threat to clinical discharge and recovery, as traveling to these facilities requires financial resources which refugees often lack.

As regards mental health, estimates suggest that 5 to 35% of international protection applicants and/or beneficiaries are survivors of torture. PTSD and related pathologies may vary between 20 and 40%, while estimates on depression vary between 30 and 70% of the refugee population[46].

[46] More information in http://www.cpr.pt/time-for-needs/

In Portugal, this is of heightened relevance, as the National Mental Health Plan remains insufficient. So as to mitigate insufficiencies, CPR cooperates with CAVITOP – Center for the Support of Torture Victims (Centro de Apoio à Vítima de Tortura), with a spatial focus on Lisbon and the Júlio de Matos hospital.

Furthermore, CPR was a partner in a transnational project entitled "TIME FOR NEEDS: LISTENING, HEALING, PROTECTING – Uma Ação Conjunta para uma Avaliação Adequada das Necessidades Especiais das Vítimas de Tortura e de Violência"[47], which ran from 2014 to October 2017. The project involved seven partners and six countries: CIR in Italy (the managing entity), ADITUS in Malta, CPR in Portugal, ECRE in Belgium, FTDA in France, GCR in Greece and Zentrum Überleben in Germany. The Time for Needs project sought to identify special needs in survivors of torture and acute violence, particularly women and children, within the scope of asylum application procedures and reception conditions, as well as to promote the benchmarking and standardization of protection practice in the European Union as applicable to this vulnerable population subset.

As the Emergency Relocation Mechanism began, the placement of refugees relocated from Greece and Italy in regions of Portugal where psychological and psychiatric care is insufficient on non-existent put these issues to the fore. There are no institutions providing care tailored to the mental health needs of refugees outside Greater Lisbon. Existing institutions require adequate training and resources on these needs. On the basis of our experience, a structured national strategy on refugee mental health is urgent. If such a strategy does not materialize, integration and self-sufficiency potential will be severely diminished.

As a concluding remark, I would like to point to the need for more support and monitoring of healthcare provision to refugees, so as to ensure acceptable standards, sufficient information and build capacity in healthcare services to provide for the needs of refugees.

[47] HOME/2014/AMIF/AG/ASYL/7836 – Co-financed by the EU. More information in http://www.cpr.pt/time-for-needs/

CHAPTER 6

Challenges for health professionals providing care for refugees and asylum seekers

ANTONIO CHIARENZA

Azienda Unità Sanitaria Locale – IRCCS of Reggio Emilia, Italy.
Chair of the Task Force Migration, Equity and Diversity.

Introduction

The influx of migrants towards Europe is an expanding and dynamic phenomenon influenced by changing politics, seasons and the evolution of major conflicts. If we look at the last three years, we notice not only that the number of migrants entering Europe has suddenly changed but also that the routes of migration have moved from Eastern to Central Mediterranean, affecting different countries and their health systems in various ways. Whereas in 2015 we saw more than a million refugees and migrants arriving in Europe [1], in 2017 the number of migrants choosing the Balkan route through Greece suddenly dropped after the Europe-Turkey statement of 18th March 2016 allowing for migrants, if declared inadmissible, to be returned to Turkey [2].

In order to understand how health systems were affected by this complex and ever-changing phenomenon, it is important to consider that the migratory influx generates the presence of different types of migrants who can be categorised according to the phase of the migration trajectory they are in and/or the type of residence status they have at that point. These phases can be divided into arrival, transit and destination, although they are not clear-cut and offer a lot of grey zones both for migrants and countries. A fourth group of migrants are those who were stranded in camps for weeks or months in typical arrival or transit locations following the closure of surrounding country borders. European countries were affected differently, depending on whether they were arrival, transit or destination countries. Yet despite the differential exposure, the situation proved similar: refugees and asylum seekers faced barriers to access adequate health services. This chapter reports on the findings of a qualitative research conducted by the HPH-Task Force Migration, Equity and Diversity (HPH-TF MED), as part of the European Union (EU) project SH-CAPAC[48]. The research aimed at investigating the challenges that refugees and health providers faced in relation to the 2015 refugee crisis and how they impacted on the accessibility of health care services.

Materials and methods

Between February and March 2016 twenty interviews and ten focus groups (FG) were carried out in ten EU countries, characterised by being primarily arrival, transit or destination countries. Interviews were conducted in The Netherlands, United Kingdom, and Austria; FGs were carried out in Belgium, Greece, Spain, Italy, Slovenia, Hungary, and Denmark. Interviews and FGs were conducted either by experts belonging to the HPH-Task Force MED or their partners[49]. Target groups were healthcare professionals

[48] *Supporting health coordination, assessments, planning, access to healthcare and capacity building in Member States under particular migratory pressure"* (SH-CAPAC). The service contract was established between CHAFEA (The Consumers, Health, Agriculture and Food Executive Agency) and a consortium of partners, led by the Escuela Andaluza de Salud Pública (Granada, Spain), the Azienda Unità Sanitaria Locale in Reggio Emilia (Italy), Trnava University in Slovakia, University of Ghent in Belgium, Jagiellonian University in Poland, Copenhagen University in Denmark, and Academic Medical Centre of the University of Amsterdam (www.sh-capac-org).

[49] Jeanine Suurmond and Vinny Mak (The Netherlands), Nazmy k. Villarroel williams, (UK), Allan Krasnik (Denmark), Ursula Trummer and Sonja Novak Zezula (Austria), Hans Verrept (Belgium), Elisabeth Ioannidi and Anna Maina (Greece), Ainhoa Rodríguez García de Cortazar, and Jaime Jiménez Pernett (Spain, Malaga), Manuel Gracia-Ramirez, Marta Escobar Ballesta and Rocío Valero Calle (Spain, Seville), Antonio Chiarenza, Benedetta Riboldi and Anna Ciannameo (Italy), Simona Jazbinšek and Uršula Lipovec Čebron (Slovenia), István Szilárd and Erika Marek (Hungary)

Table 1. Health professionals participating in FGs and interviews by country[50]

	Austria 6 interviews	Belgium 2 FGs	Denmark 1 FG	Greece 2 FGs	Hungary 1 FG	Italy 1 FG	Slovenia 1 FG	Spain 2 FGs	Netherlands 4 interviews	UK 10 interviews	Total
Medical doctor	2	2	3	4	3	1	4	3	6	3	31 (24%)
Service manager	1	4	4	1	4	2	1	1	—	—	18 (14%)
Nurse	2	2	—	6	1	3	2	2	—	4	22 (17%)
Psychologist	—	2	1	2	—	2	—	7	—	—	14 (11%)
Social worker	—	3	—	1	2	2	—	4	—	—	12 (9%)
Intercultural mediator	—	6	—	—	—	1	—	2	—	—	9 (7%)
Administrative staff	—	—	1	3	—	3	—	—	—	—	7 (5,5%)
Activist	—	1	1	1	1	—	1	—	—	3	8 (6%)
Other	1	1	—	—	1	—	—	4	—	—	7 (5,5%)
Total	6	21	10	18	12	14	8	23	6	10	128 (100%)

[50] Health professionals worked for National Health Systems (39%), NGOs (15%); Reception centres (12,5%);Government agencies (9,5%);Caritas and other charities (8,5%,), Doctors of the World (5,5%); University (5%); Red Cross (3%); Professional associations (3%)

and managers working in centres for refugees and asylum seekers, in mainstream health services (primary care services, hospitals, health promotion/ prevention), in arrival, transit and destination camps. In total 128 professionals from various organisations participated in the FGs and interviews (Table 1). Descriptive and analytical notes were taken immediately after the interviews and FGS and the outcomes were summarised by each research group in a national report. All reports were analysed and findings summarised by three researchers responsible for the overall qualitative study.[51] Findings were coded manually, categorised, and analysed, applying the six-phase approach to thematic analysis [3].

Findings

The FGs and interviews conducted made it possible to identify the main challenges that health professionals faced in providing care to refugees during their migratory trajectory, at arrival, transit and destination. Whereas health professionals experienced difficulties in ensuring access to appropriate healthcare in general, the situation proved to be particularly problematic for specific areas of care, such as mental health, childcare, sexual and reproductive care, and victim of violence care.

Challenges related to specific phases of the asylum process

Arrival

Health professionals from arrival countries (Greece, Italy, Spain) reported that refugees arrived in large numbers and usually stayed for relatively short periods of time, days or even hours. The numbers frequently overcame the capacity of existing health and other services to receive them, creating a humanitarian crisis situation. As unauthorised entrants, the legal status of newly arrived migrants was precarious, therefore refugees were in principle "irregular migrants". They often arrived without any health and personal records, health providers often lacked reliable information on the patient's situation and medical history. For example, absence of information on the vaccination status of children was a problem that was systematically reported

[51] Antonio Chiarenza (AUSL of Reggio Emilia, Italy), Hans Verrept (FPS Health, Safety of the Food Chain and Environment, Belgium), Marie Dauvrin (Université Catholique de Louvain, Institute of Health and Society, Belgium).

in the focus group discussions. During the arrival phase, healthcare professionals often had to intervene on site; it was reported that Doctors of the World and Doctors without Borders along with other NGO's were the main providers of primary healthcare in a number of EU member states. People interviewed described a situation characterised by a lack of coordination between the many different partners involved in health care provision at arrival. It was stressed that different health providers did not always act in harmony, resulting in overlapping, duplication and unmet needs. At the time that FGs were conducted this situation tended to be more problematic in countries where large numbers of asylum seekers arrived (in particular in Lesvos, Greece), because of the high number of patients to be seen. As a result, asylum seekers who needed psychosocial support, or medicines for treatment of chronic conditions often ended up in emergency units in hospitals. This increased bias and prejudice towards migrants, since they were regarded as undisciplined patients who were exploiting and misusing emergency units for problems that were not urgent. Finally, it was highlighted that in the arrival phase, often chronic diseases and immigrants' personal health plans were not taken into account.

Transit

Participants in the FGs and interviews from transit countries (Hungary, Slovenia) reported that the main concern of refugees was to continue their journey to their destination country. In this phase NGOs continued to be the main onsite providers of care, if the health problem was considered serious, refugees were taken to hospital, but they often did not complete their treatment as they wanted to continue their trip to Northern Europe. Lack of medical files continued to be a problem, so in every new health institution all of the relevant information needed to be collected again. As a result, it was reported, that treatment of chronic diseases (e.g. cancer, HIV, diabetes ...) was often inadequate. It emerged that in this situation there was little opportunity for implementing prevention and promotion programs offered by public health systems, since the focus was mainly on acute health issues and communicable diseases. Time was reported to be one of the main challenges when it came to asylum seekers in transit. For example, pregnant women were urged to take specific tests to assess their and their babies' health, however, taking into account the waiting times and protocols of EU health systems, the access to these services (e.g., gynaecological consultations, ultrasounds, and analytics) proved to be very complicated. The same challenge was reported for urgent psychological assistance and mental healthcare. People interviewed argued that the information reported by people who were in transit may be confusing, for example, saying that they intend to stay for a month but leaving two days later.

Destination

In destination countries (Austria, Belgium, Denmark, The Netherland and United Kingdom) health professionals reported that migrants remained for months or longer. It was at this stage of their journey that refugees began to attend to their health problems and required continuous health care that needed to be integrated into the regular health system. Once asylum-seekers apply for the refugee status, they gain the same entitlements to healthcare as all legal residents. However, this may imply that some services that were provided free of charge before recognition, had to be paid for by refugees. It was reported that this was the case for non-residential mental health care services in Belgium and led to financial barriers. Interviewees argued that at this stage, refugees lost much of the assistance they may have received during the previous phases. Now, the refugee would be expected to make use of mainstream healthcare services unaided. This would, in many cases, be problematic because of linguistic and cultural barriers as well as the refugee's limited health literacy and lack of knowledge of the bureaucratic and complex healthcare system. In particular, lack of provision of health service information upon arrival in the receiving country as well as poor understanding of Primary Health Care and appointment system were reported by many FG discussions. The effects of these barriers, it was argued, were aggravated by the limited cultural competence of many health providers.

Challenges related to access to health care

Legislative and administrative barriers

The legal status linked to the migration trajectory stage as well as outcomes of the asylum-seeking procedure play an important role in migrants access to health care [4]. Findings of the FGs and interviews showed that in some EU countries access to health care for many categories of migrants and refugees was limited only to emergency care, as in the case of asylum seekers in arrival camps or in identification centres, migrants in detention centres waiting for deportation, and undocumented migrants. Furthermore, the interpretation of emergency health care can be quite arbitrary, since the extent of services provided was often based on the individual decision of the health care worker treating the patient. Lack of knowledge of the different statuses and their implications for decisions taken by health providers and public social welfare services were reported by participants of the FGs and interviews.

Asylum seekers are formally owed protection, including access to health services, from the moment they apply for refugee or subsidiary protection status (Directive 2011/95/EU). In practice, however, the time taken to process documents and applications increase the frequency of situations where refugees have no effective health care coverage [5]. Many participants in the FGs/interviews pointed out that the delivery of healthcare services to asylum-seekers, refugees and undocumented migrants was seriously hampered by the complexity of administrative procedures that had to be executed to guarantee access to care. Different procedures had to be followed depending on the status of the asylum-seeker: not eligible, awaiting a decision or an appeal, asylum refused. Information on the different legal statuses of migrants and their impact on access to health care in many countries was not readily available for care providers and was inefficiently distributed to health care managers and care providers alike. In particular, health professionals argued that administrative procedures and legal limitations to the different types of care an individual patient may be entitled to, also put a strain on the care delivery process itself, since they had to explain why certain types of treatment could not be given or certain drugs could not be prescribed.

Linguistic & cultural barriers

Linguistic and cultural barriers were systematically identified by FG participants as one of the major challenges related to the refugee crisis. It was reported that in many countries there were no, or insufficient, professional interpreters or intercultural mediators available. In practice, interpreting/intercultural mediation was often carried out by NGO members (e.g. in Greece), volunteers, other refugees or professionals, who had not been trained in this domain. The negative impact of the lack of qualified interpreters on health care access for refugees and migrants is also stressed in the literature [6-9]. Many problems related to this situation were reported in FG discussions. Often healthcare had to be provided on the basis of poor communication, in some cases diagnoses and the necessity of extended treatment could not be adequately communicated. Furthermore, the impossibility of resolving linguistic barriers made it extremely difficult to handle cultural barriers that may further impede the healthcare delivery process. For example, patients coming from Syria and Iraq sometimes were reported to vehemently refuse to be treated, or have their spouses treated by a care provider of the other sex. Furthermore, health professionals affirmed that differences between the European health system and that of the migrant often led to conflicts with the patient. For example, antibiotics can easily be obtained in Syria where pharmacists have a role that is very similar to that of a MD working in primary care in Europe. To overcome these barriers, health providers participating in the FGs and interviews stressed the need to receive more training on cultural competence issues.

Lack of medical and personal information

Asylum-seekers often travel, whether in arrival, transit or destination countries, without any health and personal records. Therefore health professionals reported that they had to intervene without reliable information on the illness and treatment history of the patient. In particular, the absence of information on the vaccination status of children was a problem systematically reported by health professionals. In some countries refugee children coming from Africa and Afghanistan were systematically vaccinated as providers knew that many, if not most of them, had not been vaccinated. Problems arose when children coming from Syria, where the healthcare system used to function well, were also vaccinated, although this might not have been necessary. As no adequate systems for exchange of medical information between EU member states exist, health professionals pointed out that it was often impossible to trace patients in movement from one country to another. Even within one country, moving from one place to another, or from one type of healthcare institution to another (e.g. from a medical service in a refugee camp to a regular GP), it was reported, may entail the loss of highly relevant information on the illness and treatment history of the patient. As a result, partial and fragmented care was often provided and the right to health care not fully ensured.

Lack of organisation and coordination between services

Limited availability of services was often reported by participants of FGs and interviews, as in most countries no supplementary healthcare services were provided. Difficulties in accessing specialist services were also emphasised. Unequal distribution of facilities, lack of transportation, complex referral systems and an increased reliance on accident and emergency services for non-emergency treatment were often reported. Moreover, in countries where a lot of care is provided by volunteers or by international NGO's (e.g.: Hungary and Slovenia) the quality of care may vary greatly. Most of the international FG participants reported that the presence of different NGO's and groups of volunteers, combined with a lack of organization, might have resulted in chaotic and inadequate collaboration between the different care providers. Refugees received differing and confused information about healthcare services, such that they were unable to understand how to behave within such a complicated system.

Challenges related to specific health situations

Mental Health

FG and interview participants working in arrival camps reported that they met a huge number of refugees with mental health problems in need of psychosocial support. Rates of PTSD, anxiety and depression were especially high. This was due to the situation and to the traumatic experiences they encountered before and after their journey. In spite of all that, it was reported that there were no appropriate professionals in arrival camps, and it was difficult to access specialist therapies. To make it worse, it was reported, that repressive police and army actions further stimulated re-traumatization among refugees, which resulted in the need for many interventions by health care workers and volunteers that could otherwise have been avoided. Furthermore, extended asylum procedures, particularly when involving detention or threat of deportation, often led to psychiatric disorders. Literature shows that fear of jeopardizing an asylum application and social taboos can inhibit the disclosure of psychological symptoms. Even where permission to remain is granted, general stressors in the post-migration environment, such as insecure asylum status, financial difficulties and discrimination can damage health [5].

Language and cultural factors, were reported, as important barriers to mental health services: emotions, fears and feelings are more difficult to explain compared to other types of clinical symptomatology particularly when the language is lacking. This theme includes considerations related to the use of interpreters, but also that communication with patients entails more than simply speaking the same language. From a linguistic and cultural point of view, mental diseases represent a taboo for many communities and cause stigma and humiliation. Available literature highlights that the stigma of mental illness may provide a barrier to seeking mental care [10]. Cultural factors were also highlighted in FG discussions and interviews as potential barriers in mental health service provision. Cultural dissonance between refugee patients and service providers, it was argued, may create a barrier to access mental health services. Medical practitioners may be perceived as inflexible and insensitive to patients' needs, rushing through the consultation, thus preventing the development of trust and a rapport between doctor and patient [11, 12].

Sexual and Reproductive Health

Access to sexual and reproductive care depends on the regulations of the single country. A recent review [13] identified affordability as the major barrier to access maternal health-care. It was reported that the situation regarding financial costs for maternal health care varies among European countries; in certain countries child delivery in a hospital can be very expensive. Participants to FGs and interviews affirmed that migrant women might face legislative and bureaucratic barriers in accessing sexual and reproductive care, such as antenatal, delivery and post-natal care. In some countries they are entitled only to emergency care. Furthermore, there might be limitations regarding sex and age or pregnancy status, etc., while in other contexts undocumented migrant women cannot access health care at all. Another important barrier indicated by participants in FGs and interviews is the lack of information and familiarity with the health system on the part of refugee women. On the other hand, they said, there was a general lack of knowledge among health providers, who ignore the legal framework and the respective entitlements.

Linguistic and cultural barriers were also reported as having a negative impact on the quality of women's health care. Suboptimal care was often associated to miscommunication, lack of professional interpreters [14], and limited knowledge and information on sex and reproductive care [13]. Finally, findings of the FGs and interviews highlighted many issues surrounding sensitive topics: abortion for instance is free in certain countries, in others it requires parents' permission, and based on the political context it may become an illegal service, for which physicians may even incur some kind of punishment. Decentralization of regulations within countries was mentioned as another barrier, as well as the loss of continuity of care during the different phases of the asylum-seeking process, and the lack of free fertility care. It was reported that there was a huge debate as to whether the latter should be considered as an essential service or not.

Child Health

Refugee children and adolescents are one of the most vulnerable groups in Europe, some of them have fled persecution or war, and others have run away from poverty and destitution. There are also those who are victims of trafficking. For these reasons, mental health conditions such as post-traumatic stress disorder (PTSD), anxiety and depression are frequent [15]. Among them, unaccompanied refugee children and adolescents are particularly at risk. They live not only in a relatively difficult situation as minor refugees staying in another country, but also face other risks due to the absence of their parents, such as traumatic experiences, exploitation or abuse [16]. In Europe asylum seeking children have a right to equal access to healthcare under the same conditions as children residing in the Member State where the application for international protection is lodged [17]. However, those who are separated from their families and have no - or only temporary – residence permits are at risk of becoming undocumented children. These children can be minors arriving in Europe to be reunited with their family but not falling under the official family reunification schemes; those who entered with one or more relatives irregularly; or children born in Europe but whose parents are undocumented.

Participants of FGs and interviews reported that refugee children risked not accessing the necessary and appropriate healthcare due to legal barriers linked to age determination, as long as age influences access to care if under 18 years. As regards legal aspects, it was argued, age determination had other important consequences for young asylum seekers, in particular, it influenced access to education and determined the possibility for family reunification. The existence of different practices to assess age resulted in inequalities in access to healthcare across European Union countries. Therefore, the establishment of a standardised, human rights friendly, system of age assessment is essential [18]. Another aspect highlighted by interviewees is that lack of information on the rights to health care may be a barrier for refugee children as well as adult migrants. Health professionals pointed out that parents were often unaware of their children's right to access free health care or free education. As a consequence, refugee children might have interrupted education and this reflected on language transitions affecting their development, learning and socialization [19].

Victims of violence health

A refugee's experience of trauma and displacement may present challenges to health professionals who are unfamiliar with refugee trauma and its clinical consequences [20]. Refugees are often exposed to physical, mental and emotional torture in their native countries and a large number of women and children face violence and mental or sexual abuse during the migration trajectory. Sexual and gender-based violence (SGBV) is also a significant problem among refugee populations. Although the majority of people who experience SGBV are women, boys and men are also targets. Reports of sexual violence against women are now emerging from Syria. Not only has SGBV significant clinical consequences, it may also trigger social stigma and even exclusion of women from families and/or communities [13]. Interviewees reported that torture and SGBV survivors were often reluctant to seek treatment because they feared social stigmatisation, discrimination and further social isolation by community and family members. As a consequence, victims of violence may communicate a range of non-specific health problems in order to avoid disclosing information about their actual experience. For this reason, it was argued, clinical encounters were often complicated by inadequate communication between health professionals and patients.

Language barriers were reported by participants of FGs and interviews as having an impact upon victims of violence, preventing them from discussing their needs. Telling torture history is very difficult and painful for victims, explaining personal details and recalling the abuse is even more difficult if the listener does not share the patient's language [20]. For the issues described above, one of the most important barrier to access to health care services for torture victims is the lack of trust between clinician and patient. Difficulties in establishing a trustworthy rapport, language and cultural barriers, were stressed by FGs participants who emphasised the need to receive specific training in order to provide appropriate care for this particularly vulnerable group. In most cases, neither health practitioners nor intercultural mediators were appropriately trained to talk about violence. Furthermore, health providers often operate without specific knowledge or validated tools for the evaluation of psychological symptoms and mental disorders [21]. To this purpose, the urgent need was emphasized for practitioners and intercultural mediators to be trained in the skills needed to deal with emotionally draining situations, as well as to gain familiarity with international guidelines on providing care for victims of violence.

Discussion and conclusions

Findings of the interviews and FGs clearly show that access to healthcare for refugees and asylum seekers was not limited to the problem of acute provision at initial reception but also involved mainstream service provision. Each phase of the migratory trajectory, arrival, transit, and destination, had its peculiar challenges. European countries were affected differently by the refugee crisis, yet despite the differential exposure, the situation proved similar: asylum seekers faced barriers to access adequate health services. Refugees experienced difficulties in accessing appropriate healthcare due to legislative and administrative barriers, linguistic and cultural barriers, lack of information, organisational barriers and lack of coordination between services. Some barriers proved to be particularly problematic for specific areas of care, such as mental health, childcare, sexual reproductive care and victim of violence care.

There is an urgent need to carry out improvements in the administrative procedures, to provide information for migrants and staff on rights to health care, and promote advocacy actions to increase attention of national governments to these issues. Interpretation of legislation in situations of major influx of migrants should be relaxed. To this end, health managers have an important role in identifying and adopting administrative solutions to legislation barriers. It is necessary to consider the impact of policies of relocation, in particular, it is important that support is available for healthcare providers for asylum seekers who are in transit; this might require, for instance, that patient information is appropriately recorded and made available to new providers. To this purpose the creation of a cross-border information system is envisaged in order to enable common access to relevant medical information on asylum seekers and refugees.

Furthermore improved coordination of the various actors involved in the provision of health care for refugees and asylum seekers is essential: government agencies and ministries, Red Cross societies, NGOs, and international organisations such as the IOM and UN agencies, especially UNHCR, WHO, and UNICEF. During the refugee crisis the implementation of "contingency plans" in Sicily, involving multiple sectors and levels in order to define roles, responsibilities and effective public health interventions proved to be an effective measure in improving coordination [22]. At an organisational level, the adoption of a "whole organisational approach" (e.g.: Migrant-Friendly Hospital model), able to implement a comprehensive process of change, proved to be an effective solutions in many European countries [23]. Within the Migrant-Friendly framework, health care organisations need to develop specific programmes that address priorities for the care of refugees, for example, access to health care services can be promoted by outreach services, providing free transport to and from appointments [24]. In order to support healthcare organisation to address barriers to access and quality of care for migrants the TF-MED has developed two specific tools: a set of "standards for equity in healthcare" to measure responsiveness to diversity in healthcare provision[52] and a "resource package" to identify barriers and

[52] The Self-Assessment Tool and relevant documents are available at: http://www.hphnet.org

solutions related to accessibility of healthcare services for refugees and asylum seekers[53]. The equity standards are currently being successfully implemented in several healthcare organisations in Europe, as well as Canada and Australia.

References

(1) UNHCR, *Global trends: Forced displacements in 2015.* 2015, United Nations High Commissioner for Refugees: http://www.unhcr.org/576408cd7.pdf.

(2) UNHCR, *Regional refugee and migrant response plan for Europe. Eastern Mediterranean and western Balkans route.* 2016, United Nations High Commissioner for Refugees: Geneva.

(3) Brau, V. and V. Clarke, *Using thematic analysis in psychology.* Qual Res Psychol, 2006. **3**(2): p. 77-101.

(4) Bradby, H., et al. *Refugees and asylum seekers in the European Region - reviewing the research evidence* in *6th European Conference on Migrant and Ethnic Minority Health.* 2016. Oslo, Norway.

(5) Bradby, H., et al., *Public health aspects of migrant health: a review of the evidence on health status for refugees and asylum seekers in the European Region*, in *Health Evidence Network synthesis report.* 2015.

(6) Asgary, R. and N. Segar, *Barriers to health care access among refugee asylum seekers.* J Health Care Poor Underserved, 2011. **22**(2): p. 506-22.

(7) Morris, M.D., et al., *Healthcare barriers of refugees post-resettlement.* J Community Health, 2009. **34**(6): p. 529-38.

(8) Szajna, A. and J. Ward, *Access to health care by refugees: a dimensional analysis.* Nurs Forum, 2015. **50**(2): p. 83-9.

(9) Newbold, K.B., J. Cho, and M. McKeary, *Access to Health Care: The Experiences of Refugee and Refugee Claimant Women in Hamilton, Ontario.* Journal of Immigrant and Refugee Studies, 2013. **11**(4): p. 431-449.

(10) Ellis, B.H., et al., *New directions in refugee youth mental health services: Overcoming barriers to engagement.* Journal of Child and Adolescent Trauma, 2011. **4**(1): p. 69-85.

(11) Thomson, M.S., et al., *Improving Immigrant Populations' Access to Mental Health Services in Canada: A Review of Barriers and Recommendations.* Journal of Immigrant and Minority Health, 2015. **17**(6): p. 1895-1905.

(12) Wohler, Y. and J.A. Dantas, *Barriers Accessing Mental Health Services Among Culturally and Linguistically Diverse (CALD) Immigrant Women in Australia: Policy Implications.* J Immigr Minor Health, 2016.

[53] http://www-sh-capac.org

(13) Keygnaert I, et al., *What is the evidence on the reduction of inequalities in accessibility and quality of maternal health care delivery for migrants? A review of the existing evidence in the WHO European Region*, in *Health Evidence Network (HEN) synthesis report*, C.W.R.O.f. Europe, Editor. 2016.

(14) Yelland, J., et al., *Compromised communication: A qualitative study exploring Afghan families and health professionals' experience of interpreting support in Australian maternity care.* BMJ Quality and Safety, 2016. **25**(4): p. e1.

(15) Woodland, L., et al., *Health service delivery for newly arrived refugee children: a framework for good practice.* J Paediatr Child Health, 2010. **46**(10): p. 560-7.

(16) Derluyn, I. and E. Broekaert, *Unaccompanied refugee children and adolescents: the glaring contrast between a legal and a psychological perspective.* Int J Law Psychiatry, 2008. **31**(4): p. 319-30.

(17) Abbing, H.D., *Age determination of unaccompanied asylum seeking minors in the European Union: a health law perspective.* Eur J Health Law, 2011. **18**(1): p. 11-25.

(18) Hjern, A., M. Brendler-Lindqvist, and M. Norredam, *Age assessment of young asylum seekers.* Acta Paediatr, 2012. **101**(1): p. 4-7.

(19) Wahoush, E.O., *Equitable health-care access: the experiences of refugee and refugee claimant mothers with an ill preschooler.* Can J Nurs Res, 2009. **41**(3): p. 186-206.

(20) Crosby, S.S., *Primary care management of non-English-speaking refugees who have experienced trauma: a clinical review.* Jama, 2013. **310**(5): p. 519-28.

(21) Asgary, R. and C.L. Smith, *Ethical and professional considerations providing medical evaluation and care to refugee asylum seekers.* Am J Bioeth, 2013. **13**(7): p. 3-12.

(22) Severoni, S., S. Enkhtsetseng, and M. Dembech, *Second assessment of migrant health needs, Lampedusa and Linosa, Italy*. 2013: Available at: http://www.who.int/iris/handle/10665/107313.

(23) Bischoff, A., A. Chiarenza, and L. Loutan, *"Migrant-friendly hospitals": a European initiative in an age of increasing mobility*. World Hosp Health Serv, 2009. **45**(3): p. 7-9.

(24) Reavy, K., et al., *A new clinic model for refugee health care: adaptation of cultural safety*. Rural Remote Health, 2012. **12**: p. 1826.

CHAPTER 7

The politics of migrant health policies in Europe: attitudes, professionals and the public purse

Bernd Rechel

European Observatory on Health Systems and Policies

Introduction

There are many good reasons why migrants in Europe should enjoy the same access to health services as other groups of the population: access to health services is a basic human right and denying it violates the principle of anti-discrimination; countries in Europe have subscribed to the aim of social cohesion of which health is an important aspect; making health services more accessible to migrants might also benefit other vulnerable patient groups; and ensuring good health of migrants enables them to contribute fully to society, benefiting all.

Yet, recent work on the migrant-friendliness of health systems in Europe paints a very different picture. Legal entitlements differ vastly, as is most evident with regard to asylum-seekers and undocumented migrants. While they enjoy full legal access to health services on a par with non-migrant populations in only a handful of countries, the vast majority of European countries restrict entitlements (Médecins du monde 2017).

Why are these restrictions being put in place? Undoubtedly, some policy-makers hope for a deterrent effect of their policies, believing that restrictions would make their countries less attractive for migrants to move to, whereas providing free health care services is seen as a pull factor (Grit, den Otter et al. 2012). We know (and policy-makers may too) that this is a vain hope, as migrants are rarely motivated primarily by the desire to make use of the health systems of their new host countries (Chauvin, Simonnot et al. 2014). There are many different reasons why people migrate, such as family reunion, economic considerations, political persecution, violent conflict and natural disasters, but access to health care is not usually among the most important ones (Grit, den Otter et al. 2012).

Economic arguments are also put forward to justify restricting access. They include moral hazard, (presumed) health expenses, and the need to safeguard scarce resources (Gottlieb and Davidovitch 2017). Seemingly, it saves money not to spend scarce public resources on providing full access to health services. Denying undocumented migrants access to non-emergency health care often stems from the idea that they are free riders, taking advantage of public services without contributing to public funding (Dwyer 2004). With reductions in health budgets in many countries and the resident population facing restrictions and waiting times, some people ask how it can be justified to provide health services to newly arrived migrants. In the Netherlands, for example, Geert Wilders, the leader of the right-wing Party for Freedom, demanded that money spent to house migrants should rather be spent on cancer treatment for Dutch citizens (The Economist 2015). However, there is a growing body of evidence that suggests that restricting migrants' access to health services does not save costs (Trummer and Krasnik 2017).

It is likely that politicians do not want to appear "soft" on immigration, in particular in view of the emergence and success of anti-immigrant parties in a number of European countries, emboldened by the influx of refugees to Europe in 2015 and concerns about how many more might come. The recent success of the far-right "Alternative for Germany", becoming the party with third largest number of members of parliament in the German federal elections in 2017, is only the latest in a string of successes for populist, anti-immigrant parties, something that has been called the "march of Europe's little Trumps" (The Economist 2015). Countries where such parties have gained considerable support include Austria, Denmark, Italy, France, Hungary, Sweden, the Netherlands and Poland. This political context highlights the importance of factors outside the health system that shape policies towards migrants, including in the health sphere. This chapter explores the role of some of these factors.

What are the determinants of migrant health policies?

A number of studies in recent years have drawn attention to the vast differences that exist between countries in Europe with regard to migrant health policies and entitlements to health services for vulnerable groups of migrants, in particular asylum-seekers and undocumented migrants (Mladovsky 2009, Mladovsky, Ingleby et al. 2012, Suess, Ruiz Perez et al. 2014).

However, few attempts have so far been undertaken to explain these differences across countries. A study of health care for undocumented migrants in Europe concluded that it is difficult to pinpoint factors that could explain policy differences between countries (van Ginneken and Gray 2015). It argued that a country's history and experience of immigration plays a role, but that there are countries that are very similar in this regard, but still have very different policies towards undocumented migrants. The authors highlight the role of countries' political climate and prevailing attitudes towards migrants and immigration (van Ginneken and Gray 2015). A comparison of migrant health policies in England, Spain and Italy similarly concluded that the overall model of immigrant integration chosen by each country had a bigger influence on promoting specific health policies than the tradition as a receiving country (Vazquez, Terraza-Nunez et al. 2011).

A study of access to health care for undocumented migrants in the EU 27 also concluded that the proportion of undocumented migrants living in a country was a poor predictor of policies on access to health care (Cuadra 2012). It also found no relation between the financing system (mainly based on general taxation or social health insurance) and the levels of care to which undocumented migrants are entitled. One of the potential explanatory factors that did emerge was the existence of an (informal) labour market. In countries in which undocumented migrants enjoyed the most extensive rights to accessing health services, their pathway into irregularity was mostly related to the (informal) labour market, while countries in which undocumented migrants are largely "produced" by the asylum system (i.e. rejected asylum seekers) tended to restrict access to health services. Finally, countries relying on the regularisation of undocumented migrants (France, Italy, Spain and Portugal) tended to provide fuller access to health services (Cuadra 2012).

Attitudes of health professionals are also important in shaping migrant health policies, including their implementation on the ground. Health professionals can be biased against migrants and provide less care than they would be required, but they can also bend the rules to provide better care (Drewniak, Krones et al. 2017). A study of health care for undocumented migrants in 16 European countries, comprising semi-structured interviews with health professionals in 144 primary care services, 48 mental health services, and 48 accident and emergency departments, found that providers of emergency services pursued a pragmatic approach, reporting full access to their services for undocumented migrants, even in countries where health care is legally inaccessible for them (Dauvrin, Lorant et al. 2012).

The health strand of the 2015 Migrant Integration Policy Index (MIPEX) provides some more information on factors determining policies on migrant integration (see David Ingleby's chapter in this volume). The health strand aimed to measure the equitability of a country's policies relating to the health of migrants with regard to migrants' entitlements to health services, accessibility of health services for migrants, responsiveness to migrants' needs, and measures to achieve change. It found that 22 of 34 countries limited access to health services for undocumented migrants to emergency care, 7 countries provided access to more than emergency care, but less than for nationals, and only 5 countries (Belgium, Switzerland, France, Luxembourg, the Netherlands) provided access to undocumented migrants as for nationals (but subject to certain conditions) (IOM 2016).

A number of country characteristics were found to correlate with health strand scores: GDP per capita (adjusted for cost of living), the percentage of resident third-country nationals (i.e. non-EU/EFTA migrants), total health expenditure per capita (adjusted for cost of living), the type of health system (insurance-based or tax-based), the average score on other MIPEX strands, and whether a country was a member of the EU15 or acceded to the EU after 2000. One of the most surprising findings was that whether an EU member state belonged to the EU15 or the 13 post-2000 accession countries was a strong predictor of health strand scores. For access to health services, the best predictor of migrant health policies was whether or not the country in question was an old or a new EU member state. This suggests that post-2000 accession status is associated in its own right with restrictive policies governing migrants' access to health care, i.e. not just because of its connection with other influential variables (IOM 2016).

Country case studies

Germany

In Germany, undocumented migrants are only entitled to accident and emergency services, vaccinations and treatment of communicable diseases (Kuehne, Huschke et al. 2015, Mylius and Frewer 2015). However, entitlements are complicated by obligations to report undocumented migrants. Until 2009, health professionals in Germany were obliged to denounce undocumented migrants (Cuadra 2012). This has now changed and health professionals are no longer expected to report undocumented migrants, but the obligation still exists for public offices. This results in barriers to accessing health services, as undocumented migrants need to apply in welfare offices for a medical card to receive non-urgent care. The welfare office is obliged to report to the immigration office (Kuehne, Huschke et al. 2015, Mylius and Frewer 2015, van Ginneken and Gray 2015).

Access to health care for asylum-seekers and refugees in Germany is initially restricted for a certain period of time before regular access is granted. This "restrictionism" in German asylum policy dates back to the early 1990s and aims at reducing the (alleged) abuse of the right to asylum. The 1993 Asylum-Seekers' Benefits Act (Asylbewerberleistungsgesetz) separated welfare provisions for asylum-seekers and refugees from the general welfare system (Bozorgmehr and Razum 2015). The "waiting time" for regular access to health care (and other welfare benefits) has been subject to several amendments. In June 1997 the "waiting time" was extended from 12 to 36 months, in August 2007 it was further extended to 48 months, while in March 2015 it was reduced from 48 to 15 months (Bozorgmehr and Razum 2015). These legal restrictions are coupled with administrative barriers: service providers grant access to any type of ambulatory or specialist care only to asylum-seekers and refugees who hold a valid healthcare voucher (except for emergencies and for health care provided in reception centres). These healthcare vouchers are valid for a limited period of time, such as three months (Bozorgmehr and Razum 2015).

In addition to the expected deterrent effect of these policies, aiming to prevent asylums-seekers from moving to Germany in the first place, resource constraints were put forward by policy-makers as another argument. The aim was to reduce the resources spent on asylum seekers (Bozorgmehr, Wenner et al. 2017) in light of populist debates on the potential (financial) consequences of granting access to health care for asylum-seekers and refugees (Bozorgmehr and Razum 2015).

Yet, a study of nationally representative census data on asylum-seekers and refugees for a 20-year time period found that per capita health expenditure for asylum-seekers subject to restricted care was on average higher than for those granted regular access comparable to the general population. This suggests that the cost of exclusion from health care was ultimately higher (in terms of incident health expenditure) than granting regular access to services (Bozorgmehr and Razum 2015).

Public attitudes on migration have played an important role in influencing policies on entitlements. A study in a representative sample (n = 2524) of the German population (ages 14 years or older) between January and March 2016 found that only 22.8% agreed that it is possible for Germany to take in more unaccompanied refugee minors, whereas 45.6% disagreed. While few participants argued in support of immediate deportation of unaccompanied refugee minors in general (38.6%) or of unaccompanied refugee minors from the Middle East (35.3%), a majority advocated for immediate deportations of unaccompanied refugee minors from the Balkan region (62%) or from Africa (51.1%) (Plener, Groschwitz et al. 2017). While in 2015 in Germany "welcome culture" was a humanistic aspiration accepted by large parts of the population, in 2016 the debate shifted to issues such as better border controls and potential Islamist terrorist threats (Plener, Groschwitz et al. 2017). There might have been a shift in the public opinion about refugees, following events on New Year's Eve in Cologne, where mass sexual harassment was linked by the media to the high number of immigrants. Support for taking in asylums-seekers and refugees seems to have waned and in the German federal elections in September 2017 the far-right party "Alternative for Germany" became the party with third largest number of members of parliament.

Netherlands

In the Netherlands, undocumented migrants are excluded from buying health insurance cover because of the Linkage law (Koppelingswet), which is embedded in the 2000 Aliens Act and links "entitlement to benefits in kind, facilities and social security benefits" to the condition of lawful residence. This means that undocumented migrants have no legal right to health care services unless they can pay for them. On the basis of article 10.2 of the Aliens Act there are two exceptions to this rule: medically necessary care and care needed to protect public health (Grit, den Otter et al. 2012).

However, there are different reimbursement schemes for primary and secondary health care providers who offer health care services to undocumented migrants, operating in parallel to the usual provider payment systems. Unlike in England (see below), Dutch hospitals can provide medically necessary care to undocumented migrants who are unable to pay and have the bill covered by a special provision for "dubious debtors" in their budget. Primary health care providers can apply for money from the Linkage fund (Koppelingsfonds) run by the Ministry of Health, Welfare and Sport when they treat undocumented migrants who are unable to pay for services (Grit, den Otter et al. 2012).

Representatives from the Ministry of Health, Welfare and Sport argued that non-urgent care for undocumented migrants should not be provided immediately because this may work as an incentive for "health tourists" (used as a pejorative term for people traveling from abroad to receive free care and then returning home) (Grit, den Otter et al. 2012). However, the Dutch medical associations objected and there is now a financial reimbursement arrangement to provide care to undocumented migrants covering "de jure" nearly the same care as for Dutch citizens (Grit, den Otter et al. 2012).

Spain

In Spain there have been major changes in entitlements of undocumented migrants in the context of austerity measures following the impact of the economic crisis on the country. Previously, health care coverage for undocumented migrants was broad, linked to the expansion of the Spanish welfare state in the 1980s and the establishment of the National Health

System (NHS) in 1986, funded by general taxation and covering almost the entire population. Migrants living in Spain and registered with municipalities were granted by Law 4/2000 the same healthcare and education rights as Spanish nationals, irrespective of their legal status of residence, as long as they were registered as residents in the municipality (Vazquez, Terraza-Nunez et al. 2013, Cimas, Gullon et al. 2016, Delgado, Armesto et al. 2018). This followed the publication of an official study that showed that the cost arising from this expansion of coverage would be negligible (Grit, den Otter et al. 2012).

The severe economic crisis that affected Spain from 2009 onwards gave rise to austerity policies and attempts to reduce health expenditure. The Central Government held by the conservative People's Party passed Royal Decree Law 16 in April 2012 which, among other measures, changed healthcare entitlements. For Spanish nationals, it made coverage more explicitly linked to social security entitlements; for undocumented migrants it revoked their previous equal right to public healthcare granted by Law 4/2000 (Cimas, Gullon et al. 2016). The reform was based on a report from the Court of Auditors stating that the NHS was bearing the health-care cost of European citizens (so-called "health tourism") due to its inability to secure reimbursement (Royo-Bordonada, Diez-Cornell et al. 2013).

The Royal Decree Law, particularly its prescription to exclude undocumented migrants, was fiercely contested by political actors and civil society movements. Spanish health professionals in particular expressed their concern and many refused to comply with the law on conscientious grounds, continuing to treat undocumented migrants in NHS premises (Royo-Bordonada, Diez-Cornell et al. 2013, Cimas, Gullon et al. 2016). It is also noteworthy that attempts to set up xenophobic parties have so far flopped in Spain. Nationalism and racism are often associated with the fascist dictatorship of Francisco Franco (The Economist 2015).

As the Spanish NHS is highly decentralized, the country's regions were charged with implementing the Royal Decree Law. A comparative review of regional health policy regulations published after the enactment of the Royal Decree Law found huge variation across regions in health care coverage for undocumented migrants. While some regions applied it as intended by central government, many regions adopted legal, legislative and administrative actions to void or limit the effects of the Royal Decree Law (Cimas, Gullon et al. 2016). Six regions (Andalusia, Basque Country, Canary Islands, Catalonia, Navarra and Asturias) showed an up-front legal opposition against the Royal Decree Law, filing appeals against it to the Constitutional Court. Twelve regional health authorities passed specific legislation in order to regulate entitlement to healthcare for undocumented migrants or to modulate the consequences of the application of the Royal Decree Law, while ten regions formally established alternative administrative pathways of access to healthcare services for low-income undocumented migrants, mostly including both primary and secondary care.

When examining potential reasons for differences across regions, multivariate analysis did not show any significant relationship between the proportion of non-European residents and the score of each region. Instead, the ruling political party emerged as the main explanatory factor. Regions with a government formed by the People's Party were much more likely to comply with the legislation passed by the central government and to restrict access to health care (Cimas, Gullon et al. 2016). However, the ruling political party did not fully explain the differences, as there were five regions ruled by the People's Party that had created alternative administrative pathways to grant health care coverage to undocumented migrants (Cimas, Gullon et al. 2016).

In 2015 there was a crucial chain of elections in Spain (at local, regional and national level) and all political parties, other than the People's Party, signed an agreement to defend universal healthcare coverage (Cimas, Gullon et al. 2016). In the same year the rule was eventually relaxed, allowing undocumented migrants to freely access public health care, as the government argued, "due to the positive externalities for the public health of the population and to avoid A&E departments overload" (Delgado, Armesto et al. 2018). In fact, accident and emergency services had been struggling to cope as a result of the austerity measure (Rafighi, Poduval et al. 2016).

United Kingdom

In the United Kingdom strict regulations for undocumented migrants are related to policies for charging other groups, such as overseas visitors who are legally allowed to stay on a family-visit visa (Grit, den Otter et al. 2012). Publicly funded health care in the United Kingdom is free at the point of delivery for people "ordinarily resident". Undocumented migrants are in principle not entitled to use the National Health Service (NHS) because they are not officially resident in the country. The United Kingdom government has recently further tightened the rules of health service provision to people not "ordinarily resident" in the country and undocumented migrants are now facing increased health care costs when using primary, specialist and emergency care. In 2011, the Department of Health defined ordinarily resident as: "Living lawfully in the United Kingdom voluntarily and for settled purposes as part of the regular order of their life for the time being." The Health and Social Care Act, effective from April 2013, transformed healthcare provisions and access through a revised definition of qualifying residency, requiring that non-European Economic Area (EEA) migrants have "indefinite leave to remain" before accessing free NHS care (Rafighi, Poduval et al. 2016). The 2014 Immigration Act modified how non-EEA migrants access NHS services, ending free primary care for visitors and implementing registration and tracking at NHS registration. (Rafighi, Poduval et al. 2016).

Hospitals are required to check the residency status of patients and determine whether they fall into the category of "ordinary residents" (having the legal permission to remain in the United Kingdom). Residents without legal documents are to be charged for using NHS services. Asylum-seekers with a valid running appeal are considered "ordinary residents", but undocumented migrants do not fall in this category. However, general practitioners (GPs) have the discretion to accept any person to be fully registered as an NHS patient in order to receive free treatment.

From April 2015, a new immigration health surcharge came into force under the 2014 Immigration Act, requiring all non-EEA nationals visiting Britain for more than 6 months to pay a £200 annual surcharge (£150 for students), while short-term visitors were to pay the NHS at point of use, set at 150% of national tariffs for those from outside the EEA, from all individuals not deemed exempt (Rafighi, Poduval et al. 2016).

The British Medical Association, the United Kingdom doctors' trade union, issued a public statement of members' concerns regarding vulnerable migrants, based on humanitarian, economic, and public health arguments. It argued in favour of timely provision of appropriate care to vulnerable patients and was opposed to doctors being expected to assess patient eligibility for free NHS care (Rafighi, Poduval et al. 2016). However, its protests were largely ineffective.

Concerns over "health tourism" have played a major role in policies on entitlements of migrants in the United Kingdom. These were largely driven by campaigns against migrants in tabloids such as Daily Mail or Daily Express. Already in a 2003 government report health tourism was put forward as an argument for proposing changes to visitor regulations (Grit, den Otter et al. 2012). The former home secretary John Reid stated that "Media stories about illegal immigrants getting access to housing, legal aid or NHS care may be exaggerated, but they do reflect an underlying concern that in the past we have not been tough enough in enforcing the rules" (Grit, den Otter et al. 2012). A Home Office consultation in 2013 indicated public concern that migrant NHS entitlements were "too generous" (Home Office 2013), while ministers raised "health tourism" fears that non-residents purposefully travel to the United Kingdom to access free healthcare (Home Office 2013).

Observers argue that assertions of rampant health tourism to the United Kingdom are politically-motivated and largely baseless (Rafighi, Poduval et al. 2016). Interviewees in a qualitative study on implications of the 2014 Immigration Act and the policy to extend charges for NHS services to all migrants without right of permanent residence described concern over health tourism as "an urban myth" and "a largely fabricated problem", and rejected the idea that charging for health care was an effective tool to control immigration (Britz and McKee 2016). A more systematic study on patient movements found that, contrary to media reports, far from being a net importer of patients, the United Kingdom was a net exporter of medical travellers. In 2010, an estimated 63,000 United Kingdom residents travelled for treatment, while around 52,000 patients sought treatment in the United Kingdom (Hanefeld, Horsfall et al. 2013).

Yet, this counter-argument did not seem to affect popular beliefs. Much of the campaign in favour of leaving the European Union (EU) in the run-up to the referendum on "Brexit" in June 2016 was about limiting migration from the EU to the United Kingdom. There were also direct links to the health system, such as in the slogan of the now infamous campaign bus "We send the EU £350 million a week, let's fund our NHS instead. Vote Leave". Shortly after the referendum, leading Vote Leave proponents retreated from this promise.

There is no doubt that the persistent media campaigns against immigration and the supposed "health and benefit tourism" influenced public perceptions and, by extension, strategies and campaigns by political parties. Over the course of the 1990s and 2000s, immigration evolved to be perceived by the public as one of the most important issues, pushing other concerns into the background that arguably have a much bigger impact on people's lives (Figure 1).

Figure 1. Immigration one of the public's most important issues

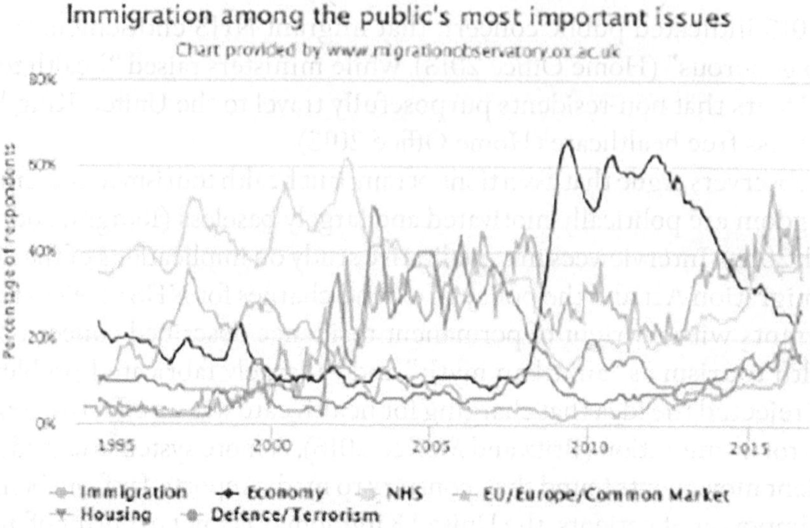

Source: Ipsos-MORI Issue Index

For much of the population, associations with migration were negative. In the 2013 British Social Attitudes Survey most respondents were in favour of reducing immigration, either "a lot" or "a little" (Figure 2).

Figure 2. Preferences for the level of immigration to Britain, 2013

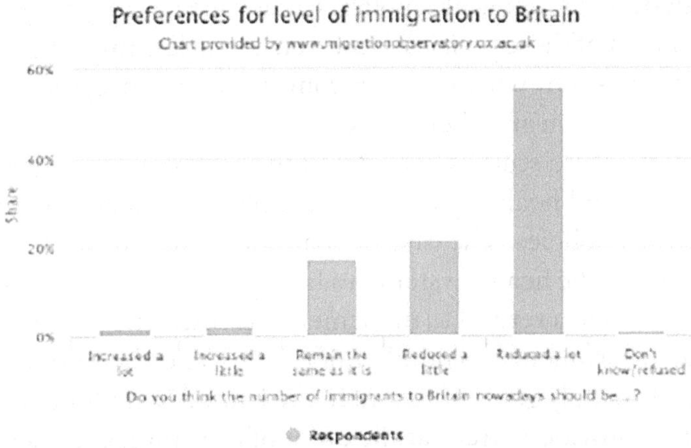

Source: British Social Attitudes Survey 2013

There was also the perception that the costs of almost all types of migrants outweigh the benefits of immigration (Figure 3), despite clear evidence to the contrary.

Figure 3. Perceived costs or benefits of immigration, 2013

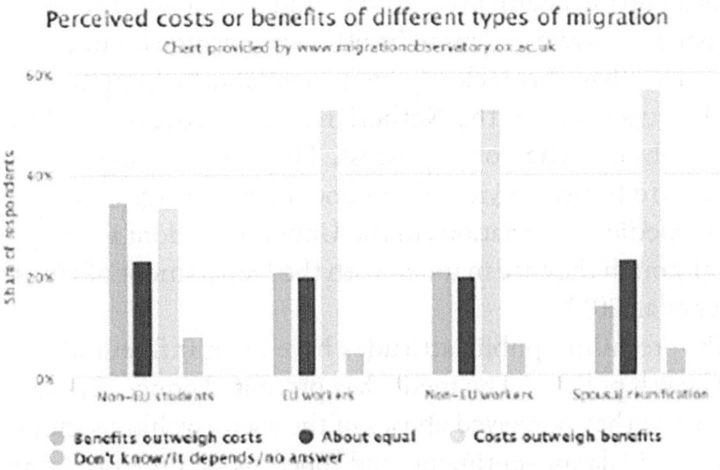

Source: British Social Attitudes Survey 2013

Conclusion

When analysing migrant health policies in Europe it is easy to get obsessed with the content of these policies. However, it is no less important to understand the processes by which policies come into existence, the main stakeholders driving them and their power relations.

The country case studies considered in this chapter suggest that the administrative and health system context plays a crucial role in shaping migrant health policies. The case of Spain illustrated how the decentralized structure of the health system in a highly divisive and contested political situation led to a refusal to implement the restrictions put forward by the central government in a number of regions, and the intended restrictions were ultimately given up again. In the United Kingdom, the fact that health care is provided "free" at the point of use "forces" policy actors to think about the circumstances under which free care should be provided to people who have not paid prospectively (Grit, den Otter et al. 2012). Health care providers are used to playing the role of prioritizing care. The situation is different in the Netherlands where payment and subsidies are actively debated. Health care providers are used to giving everyone the same level of care in the fee-for-service system. With that expectation, they fight for a good reimbursement system, even for undocumented migrants (Grit, den Otter et al. 2012).

The influence of stakeholders in the policy process also differs across countries. In Spain, health professionals and their associations have been vocal opponents to restrictions to health care coverage for undocumented migrants. They have been clearly instrumental in helping to reverse the intended restrictions. In the Netherlands too medical associations are actively involved in the policy process. They were strong supporters of equal access to health services for undocumented migrants. In contrast, the role of medical associations in the United Kingdom is comparatively limited, although they are in touch with the Department of Health (Grit, den Otter et al. 2012).

Finally, prevailing public attitudes have been influential in shaping migrant health policies. The media has promoted concerns over "health tourism" and other perceived abuses of the social welfare system, as well as broader anti-Islamic sentiments and concerns over terrorism, and there is opposition to immigration in a number of countries. Europe's "little

Trumps" (The Economist 2015) are trying to promote and take advantage of these sentiments, building on xenophobia and nationalism.

In this political climate, it might well be naïve to rely on the force of humanist arguments to improve access of migrants to health services. From the case studies presented above, cost concerns played a role in all countries, but in Germany, Spain and the United Kingdom evidence emerged that restricting access costs money rather than saves it. Yet, economic arguments in support of migrants' greater inclusion gain only scant attention (Gottlieb and Davidovitch 2017); they seem powerless against prevailing concerns over migration. This confirms that policy-making is often based on values rather than evidence. Attempts to improve access to health services for migrants in Europe would be well advised to keep this in mind.

References

Bozorgmehr, K. and O. Razum (2015). "Effect of Restricting Access to Health Care on Health Expenditures among Asylum-Seekers and Refugees: A Quasi-Experimental Study in Germany, 1994-2013." PLoS One 10(7): e0131483.

Bozorgmehr, K., J. Wenner and O. Razum (2017). "Restricted access to health care for asylum-seekers: applying a human rights lens to the argument of resource constraints." Eur J Public Health 27(4): 592-593.

Britz, J. B. and M. McKee (2016). "Charging migrants for health care could compromise public health and increase costs for the NHS." J Public Health (Oxf) 38(2): 384-390.

Chauvin, P., N. Simonnot, C. Douay and F. Vanbiervliet (2014). Access to healthcare for people facing multiple vulnerability factors in 27 cities across 10 countries. Report on the social and medical data gathered in 2013 in eight European countries, Turkey and Canada., Doctors of the World/Médecins du Monde International Network.

Cimas, M., P. Gullon, E. Aguilera, S. Meyer, J. M. Freire and B. Perez-Gomez (2016). "Healthcare coverage for undocumented migrants in Spain: Regional differences after Royal Decree Law 16/2012." Health Policy 120(4): 384-395.

Cuadra, C. B. (2012). "Right of access to health care for undocumented migrants in EU: a comparative study of national policies." Eur J Public Health 22(2): 267-271.

Dauvrin, M., V. Lorant, S. Sandhu, W. Deville, H. Dia, S. Dias, A. Gaddini, E. Ioannidis, N. K. Jensen, U. Kluge, R. Mertaniemi, I. R. R. Puigpinos, A. Sarvary, C. Strabmayr, M. Stankunas, J. J. Soares, M. Welbel, S. Priebe and Eugate study group (2012). "Health care for irregular migrants: pragmatism across Europe: a qualitative study." BMC Res Notes 5: 99.

Delgado, E. B., S. G. Armesto, J. Oliva, F. S. Martínez, J. R. Repullo, L. M. Peña-Longobardo, M. Ridao and C. Hernández-Quevedo (2018). "Spain: Health System Review." Health Systems in Transition (in press).

Drewniak, D., T. Krones and V. Wild (2017). "Do attitudes and behavior of health care professionals exacerbate health care disparities among immigrant and ethnic minority groups? An integrative literature review." Int J Nurs Stud 70: 89-98.

Gottlieb, N. and N. Davidovitch (2017). "Migrant health: putting the economic argument into the context of deservingness debates." Eur J Public Health 27(4): 591-592.

Grit, K., J. J. den Otter and A. Spreij (2012). "Access to health care for undocumented migrants: a comparative policy analysis of England and the Netherlands." J Health Polit Policy Law 37(1): 37-67.

Hanefeld, J., D. Horsfall, N. Lunt and R. Smith (2013). "Medical tourism: a cost or benefit to the NHS?" PLoS One 8(10): e70406.

Home Office (2013). Controlling Immigration – Regulating Migrant Access to Health Services in the UK. Consultation document. London, Home Office.

IOM (2016). Summary Report on the MIPEX Health Strand and Country Reports. Geneva, International Organization for Migration.

Kuehne, A., S. Huschke and M. Bullinger (2015). "Subjective health of undocumented migrants in Germany - a mixed methods approach." BMC Public Health 15: 926.

Médecins du monde. (2017). "Access to healthcare in 16 European countries." Retrieved 3 December, 2017, from https://mdmeuroblog.files.wordpress.com/2014/01/2017_final-legal-report-on-access-to-healthcare-in-16-european-countries.pdf.

Mladovsky, P. (2009). "A framework for analysing migrant health policies in Europe." Health Policy 93(1): 55-63.

Mladovsky, P., D. Ingleby, M. McKee and B. Rechel (2012). "Responding to diversity: An exploratory study of migrant health policies in Europe." Health Policy 105(1): 1-9.

Mylius, M. and A. Frewer (2015). "Access to healthcare for undocumented migrants with communicable diseases in Germany: a quantitative study." Eur J Public Health 25(4): 582-586.

Plener, P. L., R. C. Groschwitz, E. Brahler, T. Sukale and J. M. Fegert (2017). "Unaccompanied refugee minors in Germany: attitudes of the general population towards a vulnerable group." Eur Child Adolesc Psychiatry 26(6): 733-742.

Rafighi, E., S. Poduval, H. Legido-Quigley and N. Howard (2016). "National Health Service Principles as Experienced by Vulnerable London Migrants in "Austerity Britain": A Qualitative Study of Rights, Entitlements, and Civil-Society Advocacy." Int J Health Policy Manag 5(10): 589-597.

Royo-Bordonada, M. A., M. Diez-Cornell and J. M. Llorente (2013). "Health-care access for migrants in Europe: the case of Spain." Lancet 382(9890): 393-394.

Suess, A., I. Ruiz Perez, A. Ruiz Azarola and J. C. March Cerda (2014). "The right of access to health care for undocumented migrants: a revision of comparative analysis in the European context." Eur J Public Health 24(5): 712-720.

The Economist (2015). "Anti-immigrant populism. The march of Europe's little Trumps [https://www.economist.com/news/europe/21679855-xenophobic-parties-have-long-been-ostracised-mainstream-politicians-may-no-longer-be, accessed 17 January 2018]." The Economist 10 December 2015.

Trummer, U. and A. Krasnik (2017). "Migrant health: the economic argument." Eur J Public Health 27(4): 590-591.

van Ginneken, E. and B. H. Gray (2015). European Policies on Healthcare for Undocumented Migrants. The Palgrave International Handbook of Healthcare Policy and Governance. E. Kuhlmann, R. H. Blank, L. Bourgeault and C. Wendt. Houndmills, Palgrave Macmillan: 631-648.

Vazquez, M. L., R. Terraza-Nunez, S. H. S, I. Vargas, L. Bosch, A. Gonzalez, S. Pequeno, R. Cantos, J. I. Martinez and L. A. Lopez (2013). "Are migrants health policies aimed at improving access to quality healthcare? An analysis of Spanish policies." Health Policy 113(3): 236-246.

Vazquez, M. L., R. Terraza-Nunez, I. Vargas, D. Rodriguez and T. Lizana (2011). "Health policies for migrant populations in three European countries: England; Italy and Spain." Health Policy 101(1): 70-78.

CHAPTER 8

Improving the health of migrants in Europe – a challenge and an opportunity

Allan Krasnik

Professor, Department of Public Health, Danish Research Center for Migration, Ethnicity and Health, University of Copenhagen. Copenhagen, Denmark

Camilla Michaëlis

BSc in Public Health, Danish Research Center for Migration, Ethnicity and Health. University of Copenhagen, Copenhagen, Denmark

Introduction

Migration into Europe is not just an acute situation, but it is a permanent issue. Migration has always been and will always stay a central feature of human existence. Presently the global international migrants worldwide make up more than 244 million people representing about 3% of the global population. Among these 65 million are forcibly displaced which corresponds to a 41% increase since 2000. In Europe (EU) 75 million people are international migrants (8.4% of the total population). In 2016, different kinds of newcomers (asylum seekers, students and labour migrants, refugees etc) - in total about 6 million people - added about 11% to the existing migrant population, which indicates that the issue of migrant health is only partly related to the new "unplanned" migration (1).

Migration is an effect of many different factors, some could be defined as "push factors", others as "pull factors". Push factors, which are characteristics of the place of origin include problems related to poverty, climate changes, war and persecution and population growth that is not fully supported by economic development. Pull factors are mainly based on gaps between the country of origin and the country of destination in regard to education, employment, family reunification, and future life prospects in general. Mobility is generally increasing as an effect of modern developments of travel opportunities and globalization and thereby promoting migration even more than previously. We are thereby witnessing many different types of migration. Not only those of forced migration and economic migration, but also patterns of remigration back to the country of origin, circular migration involving different countries, as well as reverse economic remigration when the balance of financial developments is changing globally. Additionally, in the future we shall witness increasing environmental/climate refugees as an effect of the ongoing global climate change, especially affecting the already poor, deprived population groups in Africa and Asia.

Why a migrant health focus?

Migrants often – but not always - have different patterns of health and disease that require special attention and call for health programs which are sensitive to and tailored according to the health needs of the different migrant groups. The right to the highest attainable health is a fundamental human right according to the UN Human Rights Declaration Article 25:"Everyone has the right to a standard of living adequate for the health and well-being of himself and of his family, including food, clothing, housing, medical care and necessary social services." And the constitution of WHO states that "The enjoyment of the highest attainable health is one of the fundamental rights of every human being". The issue of equity in health as a basic principle is a key feature of many European health policy documents and according to Margareth Whitehead this principle implies that "ideally everyone should have a fair opportunity to attain their full health potential and, more pragmatically, that none should be disadvantaged from achieving this potential, if it can be avoided." (2).

In addition to these principles of rights and equity, receiving societies have an interest in sustaining migrants' health, because ill-health might hinder the ability to integrate. Challenges related to the integration of immigrants has become one of the main issues of migration policies in the European countries, but the role of health in this context has so far not been very visible in the policy debate and in policies aiming at better integration.

We do know that morbidity and mortality among migrants compared to non-migrants vary with disease categories, but also according to country of origin, ethnicity and migrant status. Consequently, we cannot treat migrants as one unit but must divide into subgroups based on country of origin, formal status and ethnicity. Migration is most often defined as the movement of a person or a group of persons from one geographical unit to another for temporary or permanent settlement"(3). But some definitions also emphasize that migration involves "A social process of change, where an individual moves from one cultural context to another for temporary or permanent settlement" (4). This means that the cultural and socio-economic aspects of migration and their significance for health should be taken into account when focusing on migrant and ethnic minority health.

There is much evidence confirming generally lower self-perceived health among migrants and their descendants compared to the majority populations in Europe (5), but we also know that lower self-perceived health is associated with lower socio-economic status among immigrant groups as well as among the majority populations. In many studies socio-economic status measured as level of education, employment or income is taken into account in the analyses, and the findings in these studies often show that the effect of migration or ethnicity is reduced, but rarely totally eliminated (6). This means that social factors do play a clear role in the context of health among migrants, but being a migrant has an effect of its own. How social integration and health actually interact as part of the life-course of migrants is still unclear.

Integration and health

A recent literature review (not published) looked into the European literature on the relationship between integration of migrants and health and found a limited number of publications. The studies examined different concepts related to migration and ethnicity (including immigrant, migrant, transient, refugee, ethnic minority), as well as concepts of social integration, acculturation, socio-economic factors and assimilation. Many types of indicators were identified in the studies, including acculturation, assimilation, social integration, duration of stay, age at arrival, education, occupation and language skills that are expected to be directly related to the process of integration. Health issues were documented in the form of health behaviours, disease, sickness absence, reproductive health, self-reported health, quality of life and mortality. This is illustrated by selected publications in the following.

Regarding health behaviours the studies mainly looked into dietary habits, overweight, physical activity and smoking and found that duration of stay as well as language skills were associated with these variables (7-14). A few studies also identified acculturation and social integration as important factors without being able to identify the causal directions and processes (15-16). A Dutch study by de Munter et al (12) demonstrated significant associations between socioeconomic position and leisure time physical activity as well as active commuting among immigrants as well as among the Dutch population. A Swedish study provided clear evidence on the association between the level of language proficiency and leisure time physical activity (15). A German study on the association between acculturation and smoking among pregnant immigrant women from Turkey found that smoking increased with increasing acculturation level, measured by an acculturation scale, by length of stay, and by German language proficiency (13). The chance of being a smoker was significantly higher among Turkish women with a length of stay of ≥20 years compared to 0–4 years; among Turkish women with good/very good language skills compared to none/minor skills; and among Turkish women with high levels of acculturation compared to low levels. Similar changes in smoking behavior by length of stay among Turkish immigrants were found in another German study. With each year spent in Germany, smoking prevalence increased among Turkish women whereas the prevalence among men slightly decreased. Among Eastern European immigrants no significant changes were apparent (14).

The literature on health has mainly looked into cardiovascular diseases, mental health issues and self-reported health, and studies have demonstrated associations with acculturation, duration of stay, social integration and employment. A Danish study by Hempler et al (17) showed higher rates of cardiovascular diseases by duration of stay among older immigrants from Turkey and Pakistan when compared with persons of similar age among the Danish born citizens even after control for socio-economic status. A Spanish study on the role of employment for mental health provided evidence of a strong effect of transition from employment to unemployment among immigrants in Spain whereas no effect of continuous unemployment was found when comparing with those migrants that were continuously employed (18).

The role of acculturation for depressive symptoms was examined in a German study that categorized Turkish immigrants into 4 groups: assimilated, integrated, marginalized and separated according to the level of orientation towards the host culture (high or low orientation) versus the culture of origin (19). They found that the average level of depressive symptoms were significantly higher among the marginalized and separated groups (with low orientation towards the host culture, but low or high orientation towards the culture of origin) than among those who were categorized as integrated (high orientation towards both host culture and culture of origin). Another German study assessed the association between acculturation and health-related quality of life among persons with a Turkish migrant background in Germany using a similar categorization into four groups (integration, assimilation, separation and marginalization). They found that compared to integration, separation was associated with poorer physical and mental health among those who immigrated in adulthood whereas marginalization was associated with poorer mental health in descendants of migrants (20).

These findings – although still characterized by limited evidence – do seem to indicate that the process of integration as an immigrant in Europe is somehow associated with health issues, either because integration is facilitated by good health (those who are healthy are in a better shape to learn the new language or stay employed) or because good integration influences the health of migrants in a positive way (those who are well integrated are less likely to develop health problems such as depression). Integration processes seem to matter – perhaps by shaping better conditions for staying healthy or for coping with disease. But what do we know about the role of integration policies for the health of migrants?

A few studies have looked into the possible effect of policies on health by comparing health of migrants in European countries with different kinds of migration policies. Ikram et al defined three kinds of policies:

Exclusionist policies (Denmark) compared to assimilationist policies (France) and inclusive policies (The Netherlands) (21).The analysis demonstrated a higher over-all mortality and CVD mortality as a possible effect of the exclusionist policies when comparing similar ethnic minority groups across the three types of countries. Malmusi et al (22) used the MIPEX scoring based on an index combining different integration policies for each country (23) and also showed that immigrants in exclusionist countries reported worse health than those in assimilationist and multicultural countries when applying the MIPEX scores. When comparing health status among migrants with that of majority populations the health inequalities in the exclusionist countries were also larger - even after controlling for socio-economic status.

The health effect of different phases of the trajectory of migrants

The health of migrants – like the health of all people – is an effect of a multitude of factors characterizing and influencing each individual during a life-course. The trajectory of migrants can be seen as a process consisting of different phases which each may strongly affect health. These include basic conditions in the country of origin such as educational possibilities, dietary habits, housing conditions, climate, the level of health care services etc. Some conditions might be leading to migration, but also to health problems (poverty, war, discrimination and violence). Similarly, the process of migration may involve traumatic and stressful experiences, and finally the postmigration factors are playing a clear role – right from the arrival in the destination country. The postmigration situation for migrants may be directly affected by the integration policies as indicated above, but these policies need to take account of the previous health hazards during the course of migration in order to maximize the effect of the integration policies, programs and direct health interventions. Without taking the effect of previous health hazards into account, the social and health services in the destination countries are not able to fulfill their tasks.

This also implies that it is not possible to handle integration and migrant health issues as if migrants were a homogeneous population group with similar needs and potentials. The public discourse and some of the policy decisions often seem to reflect generalizations and myths that are not taking into account the large variety of characteristics of the different population groups of concern. Country of origin or religion often plays a much too dominating role for the way migrants are perceived and handled in the receiving countries (24). Issues such as migration status (e.g. asylum seeker, refugee, labour migrant, family reunited, etc), family situation, community belonging, educational background, and ethnic values and practices are often invisible or forgotten in the data sets, the media debate, the policy decisions and the service programs. Instead, there is a need for much closer collaboration and coordination between countries, the different public sectors, the private organizations and the civil societies in order to take account of the multifactorial determinants of health and the role of intersectionality (interaction of different characteristics of the individuals) for migrant health (25).

This is in full accordance with the Council of Europe Recommendation on mobility, migration and access to health care (26). The Council states that governments should do their best, having regard to the organization, general principles and financial capacities of the social security system of the member state concerned, to provide migrants with adequate entitlements to use health services which meet their needs. Unnecessarily complex or laborious procedures for obtaining health service provision should be simplified. The Council recommends that national governments should enter into partnerships with all stakeholders and actors concerned, as well as with migrant organisations: change at each level needs to be supported by associated changes at all other levels. As it has been clearly stated by Ingleby (27) there is a strong need for an integrated, intersectional, multivariate and multilevel approach!

When organizing social and health service delivery it is crucial to ensure the availability, accessibility, acceptability, and quality of services (AAAQ) for all kinds of migrants taking into account their different characteristics, needs and potentials which have been influenced by their life course experiences. Formal factors like legal conditions and financial barriers need special attention when considering the different migrant groups, but also informal issues, which are both patient- and system related, play a big role in order to ensure early interventions and high quality service, promoting integration and health of all kinds of migrants. The choice and development of the kinds of services provided need to consider existing evidence on potentials and challenges, both in relation to the role of inclusive mainstream programs, and dedicated interventions with a special focus on the needs and characteristics of the different migrant groups.

The workforce involved needs the relevant and sufficient cultural and diversity competences and staff with special tasks in relation to cultural mediation are sometimes needed. Information systems are presently generally underdeveloped without sufficient disaggregated data, and the necessary flow of information across countries and across services is difficult and often non-existent due to technical limitations and ethical issues regarding confidentiality, but also just due to lack of refinement and sensitivity to the specific categorizations of migrants required and to the problems that need special attention. And last, but not least there is a strong need for leadership and governance ensuring development and management of services and programs that do take into account that European populations are increasingly diverse, and that services and staff need to reflect and respect these changing population compositions in order to ensure human rights for everyone living in the country.

General benefits of focusing more on migrant health in research, policy and practice

The focus on migrants is important for the health and wellbeing of migrants themselves, but also for society in general. Lack of integration may lead to economic and social problems of concern to everyone, lack of interventions towards preventable health issues can be costly in the longer perspective and so is insufficient care for those who are in need. But besides, we can learn important lessons on health and disease from migrant health. Important evidence on determinants of health derives from studies of migrants who have been subject to changes in their life conditions due to migration – sometimes demonstrating better health at arrival than the majority population in their country of destination and often showing changing patterns of disease as an effect of the new life conditions. Different coping strategies and effects of ill-health can be identified through comparative studies of migrants versus other population groups and thereby provide insight in new ways of handling health issues by communities and individuals. Developing comprehensive and effective, innovative social and health programs for migrants might also lead to new knowledge and experiences on how to best handle social challenges and health problems for other population groups than migrants.

Conclusions

Migration is an essential and unavoidable dimension of human history that has mainly been benefitting mankind. The largest stock of migrants in Europe have been here for years and arrived as legal migrants for work or education, or have been accepted as citizens, refugees or family reunited. The recent influx of migrants to Europe has initiated strong political and media focus, but should be seen in the context of the much larger already existing migrant and ethnic minority populations and could be considered being a political rather than a migration crisis. Issues of social integration and employment of immigrants is also receiving more attention, but the well-known links between "socio-economic factors" and "health" seems to be overlooked when integration of migrants is the issue. Better migrant health policies should therefore be motivated not only by human rights and equity goals, but also by issues of integration, both in the context of promoting integration through improvement of health of migrants, but also in regard to promoting health through successful integration.

A focus on migrant health is therefore highly motivated in regard to policy, practice and research – not only for better integration and health for the migrants, but also in order to provide fruitful lessons for public health in general. Diversity sensitive policies and practices are needed for the population at large, and innovations that prove effective for migrants in terms of social integration and health might very well inspire the development of social and health programs for many other population groups in need of inclusive and qualified interventions and support.

References

(1) World Health Organization Regional Office for Europe. Strategy and action plan for refugee and migrant health in the WHO European Region [Internet]. Copenhagen: World Health Organization; 2016 p. 1-29. Available from: http://www.euro.who.int/__data/assets/pdf_file/0004/314725/66wd08e_MigrantHealthStrategyActionPlan_160424.pdf

(2) Whitehead M. The Concepts and Principles of Equity and Health. International Journal of Health Services. 1992;22(3):429-445.

(3) United Nations. General Assembly - International migration and development Report of the Secretary-General [Internet]. 2016 p. 1-21. Available from: http://www.un.org/en/development/desa/population/migration/generalassembly/docs/A_71_296_E.pdf
(4) Syed H, Vangen S. Health and migration: A review - NAKMI papers 2/2003. Oslo: AKMI - Norwegian Center for Minority Health Research; 2003.
(5) Nielsen SS, Krasnik A. Poorer self-perceived health among migrants and ethnic minorities versus the majority population in Europe: A systematic review. Int J Public Health. 2010;55(5):357–71.
(6) Dinesen C, Nielsen S, Mortensen L, Krasnik A. Inequality in self-rated health among immigrants, their descendants and ethnic Danes: examining the role of socioeconomic position. Int. J. Public Health. 2011;56(5):503-514.
(7) Jayaweera H, Quigley MA. Health status, health behaviour and healthcare use among migrants in the UK: Evidence from mothers in the Millennium Cohort Study. Soc Sci Med [Internet]. 2010;71(5):1002–10. Available from: http://dx.doi.org/10.1016/j.socscimed.2010.05.039
(8) Wandel M, Råberg M, Kumar B, Holmboe-Ottesen G. Changes in food habits after migration among South Asians settled in Oslo: The effect of demographic, socio-economic and integration factors. Appetite. 2008;50(2–3):376–85.
(9) Gualdi-Russo E, Zaccagni L, Manzon VS, Masotti S, Rinaldo N, Khyatti M. Obesity and physical activity in children of immigrants. Eur J Public Health. 2014;24(SUPPL.1):40-6.
(10) Martin-Fernandez J, Grillo F, Tichit C, Parizot I, Chauvin P. Overweight according to geographical origin and time spent in France: A cross sectional study in the Paris metropolitan area. BMC Public Health. 2012;12(937):1-14.
(11) Iversen T, Ma CTA, Meyer HE. Immigrants' acculturation and changes in Body Mass Index. Econ Hum Biol [Internet]. 2013;11(1):1–7. Available from: http://dx.doi.org/10.1016/j.ehb.2012.02.003
(12) de Munter J, Agyemang C, Brewster L, Stronks K, van Valkengoed I. The association of leisure-time physical activity and active commuting with measures of socioeconomic position in a multiethnic population living in the Netherlands: results from the cross-sectional SUNSET study. BMC Public Health. 2012;12(815):1-10.
(13) Reiss K, Breckenkamp J, Borde T, Brenne S, David M, Razum O. Smoking during pregnancy among Turkish immigrants in Germany - are there associations with acculturation? Nicotine Tob Res. 2015;17(6):643–52.
(14) Reiss K, Schunck R, Razum O. Effect of length of stay on smoking among Turkish and Eastern European immigrants in Germany - Interpretation in the light of the smoking epidemic model and the acculturation theory. Int J Environ Res Public Health. 2015;12:15925–36

(15) Jönsson L, Palmer K, Ohlsson H, Sundquist J, Sundquist K. Is acculturation associated with physical activity among female immigrants in Sweden?. J of Public Health. 2012;35(2):270-277.
(16) Méjean C, Traissac P, Eymard-Duvernay S, Delpeuch F, Maire B. Influence of acculturation among Tunisian migrants in France and their past/present exposure to the home country on diet and physical activity. Public Health Nutr. 2009;12(6):832–41.
(17) Hempler N, Larsen F, Nielsen S, Diderichsen F, Andreasen A, Jørgensen T. A registry-based follow-up study, comparing the incidence of cardiovascular disease in native Danes and immigrants born in Turkey, Pakistan and the former Yugoslavia: do social inequalities play a role?. BMC Public Health. 2011;11(662):1-9.
(18) Robert G, Martíenz JM, García AM, Benavides FG, Ronda E. From the boom to the crisis: Changes in employment conditions of immigrants in Spain and their effects on mental health. Eur. J. Public Health 2014;24:404–409.
(19) Morawa E, Erim Y. Acculturation and depressive symptoms among Turkish immigrants in Germany. Int. J. Environ. Res. Public Health 2014;11:9503–21.
(20) Brand T, Samkange-Zeeb F, Ellert U, Keil T, Krist L, Dragano N, et al. Acculturation and health-related quality of life: results from the German National Cohort migrant feasibility study. Int. J. Public Health 2017;62:521–9.
(21) Ikram U, Malmusi D, Juel K, Rey G, Kunst A. Association between Integration Policies and Immigrants' Mortality: An Explorative Study across Three European Countries. PLOS ONE. 2015;10(6):e0129916.
(22) Malmusi D, Palència L, Ikram UZ, Kunst AE, Borrell C. Inequalities by immigrant status in depressive symptoms in Europe: the role of integration policy regimes. Soc. Psychiatry Psychiatr. Epidemiol. 2017;52:391–398.
(23) International Organization for Migration. Summary Report on the MIPEX Health Strand and Country Reports [Internet]. Geneva: International Organization for Migration; 2016 p. 1-103. Available from: https://publications.iom.int/system/files/mrs_52.pdf
(24) Bhopal R. Terminology and classifications for ethnic and racial groups; the centrality of census and population registers. In: Migration, ethnicity, race, and health in multicultural societies. Oxford University Press; 2014. 33–61.
(25) Ikram U. Social determinants of ethnic minority health in Europe [PhD thesis]. Faculty of Medicine (AMC-UvA); 2016.
(26) Council of Europe. Recommendation CM/Rec(2011)13 of the Committee of Ministers to member states on mobility, migration and access to health care [Internet]. Council of Europe: Committee of Ministers. 2011. Available from: https://search.coe.int/cm/Pages/result_details.aspx?ObjectID=09000016805cbd6d
(27) Ingleby D. Ethnicity, Migration and the 'Social Determinants of Health' Agenda*. Psychosocial Intervention. 2012;21(3):331-341.

CHAPTER 9

Migrants and health: Current status in Norway

BERNADETTE. N. KUMAR
Norwegian Center for Migration and Health, Norway[54]

Introduction

For humankind, migration as well as health have existed since time immemorial though not often explored together until recent times. The "Migration Period" of the Middle Ages (300-700 AD) resulted in dramatic changes in the architecture of populations in Europe Many would argue that we are in the midst of a similar "Migration Period" of our times (1). This article will briefly outline some terms and definitions and explore the association between migration and health. Further, migrants to Norway and their health status will also be described to illustrate the associations made earlier. As it is beyond the scope of this article to cover all the relevant areas some popular migrant health myths will be dealt with. Finally, the article will summarize the main challenges being faced, the opportunities and the way forward.

[54] "Butterflies have always had wings; people have always had legs. While history is marked by the hybridity of human societies & the desire for movement, the reality of most of migration today reveals the unequal relations between rich & poor, between North and South, between whiteness and its others." – Harsha Walia, Undoing Border Imperialism

Migrant Health

Human migration can be defined in many ways but a very simple description is the geographic movement of human beings that is either permanent or semi-permanent in nature. This migration can be either forced; encompasses refugees and human trafficking or voluntary; migrant workers, students and family union etc.

While the term migrant is often used in communicating to a broad audience, the complexities of the many subgroups under this terminology are often lost. Refugees are a subset of the wider migrant term. The United Nations High Commissioner for Refugees (UNHCR) reports 244 million international migrants of which 67.7 million people of concern (refugees, asylum seekers, internally displaced persons and stateless persons) worldwide of which more than 17 million are refugees (2). However, most of the migration takes place within a country and not across borders with nearly 1 billion people on the move.

Changing demographics in nation states around the world have given way to homogenous populations paving the way for diversity. Diversity as a virtue in a nation is an idea from the rise of modern democracies in the 1790s, where it kept one faction from arrogating all power (but this was not quite the modern sense, as ethnicity, gender, sexual identity, etc). Along with globalization of economy, technology and transportation, diversity is a major driver for migration.

Many are familiar with WHO's definition of health as contained in its constitution: "Health is a state of complete physical, mental and social well-being and not merely the absence of disease or infirmity" (3).

Over the years, while demographers and social scientists have worked steadily with migration research, as have health researchers with health, Migration and Health *per se* has often fallen between the cracks between these two groups of professionals. The interest in Migration and Health has gradually evolved, over the years, from the interest of a select few in exotic disease to main stream health care. It can be best described in the following table (4):

Table 1. Phases in the development of interest in the health in migrants

PHASES	FOCUS	EXAMPLE
1. Exotic disease phase	Early interest in the unusual or seldom occurring diseases of minority ethnic groups	Infections
2. Biological Difference	The study of biological differences, with a focus on genetically inheritable diseases	Hemoglobinopathies
3. Population Differences	Population patterns of disease; Group comparisons with White as majority	Somatic Diseases/ Mental Health.
4. Adapting Health Care to Diversity	Adapting health-care policy, research and services to meet the needs of ethnic minority groups. Challenge: Trying to ensure that the health-care system as a whole is primed to meet the challenges of multicultural health care.	Access to health Systems Discrimination Intervention Studies

Mark Johnson (1984) (4)

Another important aspect of both Migration and of Health is that they are both dynamic and not static in nature. Therefore, it is very important to consider migration in phases that can be cyclical. These phases are: Predeparture (in the country of origin), Transit (the journey - the interim country of destination), Post arrival (in the country of destination), Return (to country of origin). While these phases are well documented what has changed over the recent years is that the transit period could take several years and become a semi-permanent situation for many (5).

Migration to Norway – Who? Why? Where?

While migration to Norway is not a new phenomenon, prior to 1945 the numbers were few and migrants came mainly from Nordic countries and Europe. After 1945, the migrant waves followed world events as seen by refugees from Chile and Vietnam in the 70s, from Balkans in the 80s and more recently the Poles after 2005. Immigrants and Norwegian-born with immigrant parents now account for 16.8% of Norway's population (6) compared to 1% of the population in 1970. Before 2004 refugees were among largest group of migrants in Norway whereas today, 45% are migrant workers and their families and 23% have refugee backgrounds, including asylum seekers (6).

The migrant population is rather young with half the population being in the age group 20-44 years and only 5% are over 66 years. Among the Norwegian born with immigrant parents, 85 percent are under 20 years of age (6). About 48% of the immigrant population comprises women, but this varies with country of origin. Men are in overwhelming majority among immigrants from the new EU countries, Poland and Lithuania, as well as newly arrived refugees from Afghanistan and Iraq (6).

Migrants to Norway come from over 200 countries and territories and over 50% originate from Europe. The largest groups originate from the following countries; Poland, Lithuania, Sweden, Somalia, Germany, Pakistan, Iraq, Russia, England, Philippines, Iran, Thailand, Vietnam, Bosnia and Afghanistan (6).

Norway is no exception from the rest of Europe with the number of asylum applications in Norway having increased significantly from 11,480 in 2014 to 31,145 (6926 women) in 2015. One third of these (9,793) are children (under 18 years) among whom 2,505 are girls. Most came from Syria (10,267) followed by Afghanistan (6,625), Iraq (2,921), Eritrea (2,893), Iran (1,253) and Stateless (1,096). A significant number of unaccompanied minors mainly boys (5,297) arrived in 2015 (7).

The majority of migrants have lived in Norway for less than 5 years. A relatively large proportion among some immigrant groups have no or little education. Immigrants are overrepresented in lower income groups and have lower employment rates than the Norwegian population. These factors put immigrants at a disadvantage in society and impact their health as well. Future projections predict that the total number of immigrants in Norway will grow from 0.55 million in 2012 to 1.3 million in 2050, so neither migrants nor migration is likely to disappear.

Are health services prepared for the rapidly increasing diversity in Norway?

With the steady increase in the number of migrants over recent years, the evidence on the health of migrants has surely but slowly been generated. Though the evidence is fragmented and there are gaps, it tells us that the health of migrants reflects their heterogeneity. There are significant variations in disease prevalence and risk factors across gender, ethnic and age groups. A higher burden and greater risk of lifestyle- and diet-related disorders, mental health problems, infectious diseases and complications of reproductive health were observed among certain groups. Immigrants from low- and middle income countries have poorer health compared to immigrants from Western countries and Norwegians (8-10).

Many may concur with the view that Norway is now in the fourth phase of the development of Migration Health and this phase is about adaptation and how to respond to diversity. Though migration and migrants are not new to Norway, the first ever National Strategy on Immigrant Health was launched as recently as 2013. This strategy is based on recent White Papers to the Norwegian Parliament (Meld. St.16, 2010-201; Melt. St. 6, 2011-2012), which clearly emphasizes addressing the social determinant of health, such as: employment, good education, better housing and better living conditions, in order to reduce the existing health differences. The key elements of the strategy can be summarized in the main purpose as given below.

The State shall ensure that:

- *Health care providers at all levels have basic knowledge about various migrant groups' disease incidence and the cultural challenges related to ensuring equitable healthcare services.*
- *Health care providers at all levels shall facilitate good communication with non Norwegian speaking patients. This includes securing a qualified interpreter when the need arises.*
- *Healthcare services must be equipped with updated knowledge about migrants' health and their use of the healthcare service, as well as use the knowledge in the development of services.*

What should health services be prepared for? Dispelling the migrant health myths

The discussion and debate around what health services should be prepared for varies and with good reason. However often these discussions, in particular, in the public domain, are based not on proven hypotheses or evidence but on a number of migrant health myths.

But before tackling some of the most common myths it is worth considering some of the well- known and established hypothesis about migrant health. To discuss these in depth is beyond the scope of this article, but among those worth mentioning are those that explain better health of migrants compared to host populations; *Healthy migration' effect* (those with resources to migrate and re-establish themselves may be more resourceful, also health wise),*'Salomon' effect* (those who or old/sick may have a propensity to return to their country of origin therefore mortality among migrants appears to be lower than it is).On the other hand *'Acculturation'* (migrants may adopt healthy/unhealthy behaviours common in their destination country) or the *'Social causation'* (it may be socially burdensome to be a migrant, discrimination has negative health effects) might explain worsening health of migrants over time.

MYTH 1 – Migrants are Unhealthy

Notwithstanding the actual health status and health outcomes for migrants, there is no dearth of myths and the most common one is that the health of migrants is much poorer because they are carriers of disease, have poor health habits and believe in mysterious health practices.

In Norway, all individuals age 25-79 in 1990-2012 were included in our study (11) and we studied 451,000 deaths in around 4.4 million individuals. Immigrants accounted for around 15% of the individuals (but fewer observation years) and experienced 18,400 deaths. Discrete time regression models with time-varying covariates were used to assess the relative death risk between hosts and various immigrant groups, and to facilitate comparisons across models, marginal effects were calculated. We found that immigrants in Norway have lower mortality than hosts and sociodemographic factors play an important role for immigrants' survival advantage. (See figure 1 below).

Figure 1. Death risks (ORs) by country group origin

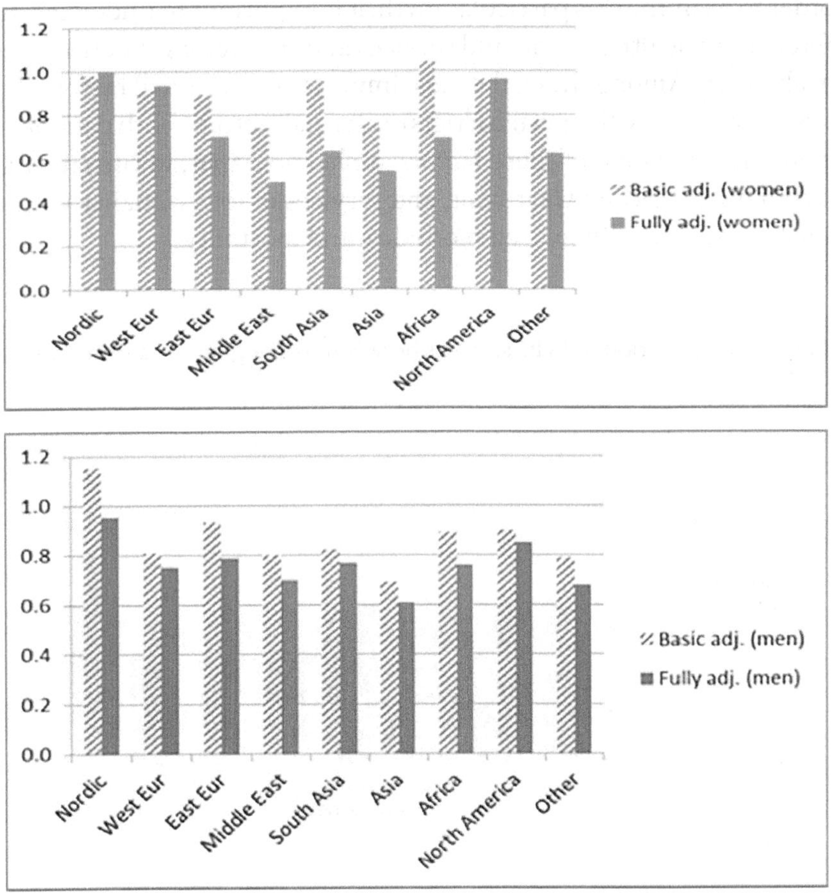

Note. The host population is the reference category (OR = 1). Age group and calendar period represent basic adjustment (shaded), whereas full adjustment also includes education, marital and parental status (full).

Although mortality varied substantially between migrant groups according to country of origin, no group had a higher death risk than the host population after adjustments for sociodemographic factors. However, the convergence in mortality for hosts and immigrants with increasing duration of residence suggests that 'healthy migration' and negative acculturation effects may counteract each another.

MYTH 2 – Migrants are a burden on Health Systems

In order to examine this particular myth, it is important to understand the differences in health systems and services and the factors affecting access to health care. Among these, the most important are; formal factors (legal rights; entitlements, financial barriers), informal factors (both patient- and system related). Some of these factors are barriers that, in turn, result in delays in diagnosis and treatment, and services of lower quality with the ultimate outcome of increased morbidity and mortality.

Figure 2. Utilization of PHC services between Norwegians and Immigrants

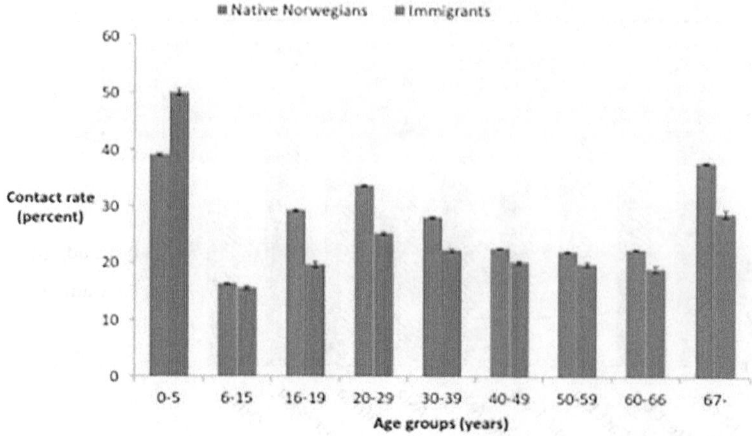

Figure 2 shows the utilization of PHC services between Norwegians and Immigrants in a population-based study from registry data that included the entire population. The findings showed that in all age groups there was lower utilization of PHC services among immigrants except in the under 5 age group. (12). Another study by Elstad et al studied use of hospital services and found lower rates of admission to hospitals (13). Immigrants' lower utilization could be appropriate if it reflects better health among immigrants, however it could also be due to barriers for utilization of services such as communication, inability to navigate the system among others.

MYTH 3 – Health Care Reason for Migration

Another popular myth in Europe is that generous social rights attract more migrants. However, Figure 3 shows the recent migration to Europe from Syria and it is clearly evident that the largest proportion are in the neighbouring countries. According to UNHCR, 40% moved to neighbouring country.

Figure 3. Recent migration to Europe from Syria

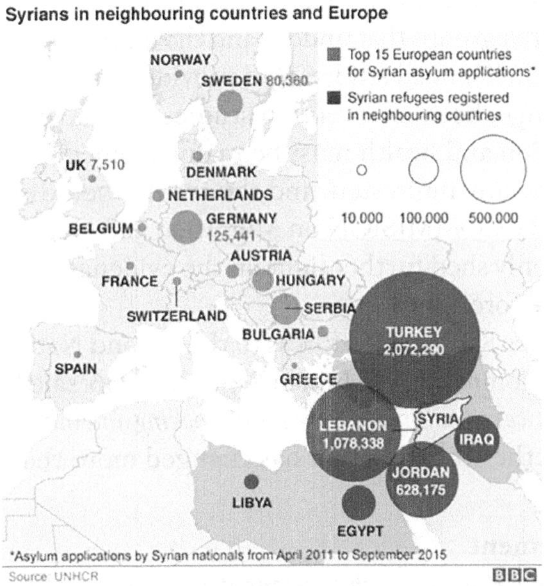

Conclusion

'Migration is not a problem to be solved but a situation to be managed' (IOM). The changing context of diversity with the changing composition of populations must pay attention to migrants as an important sub group. Although medical/nursing management of a particular disease might be the same globally, the biggest challenges lie in the context both of the patient and the situation - establishing patient needs, ideas and expectations related to a particular situation. It is key to recognise individual needs and resources, responding to these appropriately and timely, challenging the ability to make appropriate decisions consistently. It is about being able to deal with increasing diversity in the context of a society that focuses heavily on efficiency, tighter regulations and standardised solutions (14, 15).

The way forward cannot be a path that does not involve the migrants. Migrant involvement will raise the potential for improving health through empowerment of the users. Adapting services to the needs of migrants is essential through building skills and competence of health providers and strong clinical institutions to develop best practice. In order to reach the sustainable goals of universal coverage that will include migrants we must continue to build the evidence base. This must be done by; building and fostering research groups that understand the migration process as well as migrants' health. We need studies that provide valuable insight into how to achieve change, both intervention studies and health system studies. Finally, migration and health must be mainstreamed in all research, not just for the specially interested, and the results well disseminated. The UCL – LANCET COMMISION on Migration and Health 2016-2018 will hopefully not only shed further light on the evidence base but also bring this topic to the forefront.

Martin Luther King in an address to the Second National Convention of the Medical Committee of Human Rights in 1966: said *'Of all the forms of inequality, injustice in health care is the most shocking and inhumane.'* It remains to be seen whether this situation has changed more than 50 years later.

Acknowledgement
Thanks to Prabhjot Kour, research assistant at NAKMI, for technical support with regard to the references. NAKMI's goal is to be the nexus for minority health, through research, education, training, capacity building and dissemination of research and information regionally, nationally and internationally.

References:

(1) Kumar B, Siem H, Haavardsson I, Winkler AS. Migrant health is global health. Tidsskr Nor Laegeforen. 2017, doi: 10.4045/tidsskr.17.0656
(2) The United Nations High Commissioner for Refugees (UNHCR). Global trends: Forced displacement in 2016. 2017.
(3) World Health Organization (WHO). Constitution of WHO: principles. Available from: http://www.who.int/about/mission/en/

(4) Mark Johnson 1984
(5) Gushulak BD, Weekers J, MacPherson DW. Migrants and emerging public health issues in a globalized world: threats, risks and challenges, an evidence-based framework. Emerging Health Threats Journal. 2010; 2: e10.
(6) Statistics Norway. Migrations. 2017. Available from: http://www.ssb.no/en/befolkning/statistikker/flytting
(7) The Norwegian Directorate of Immigration (UDI). Statistics and analysis: Statistics on immigration. Available from: https://www.udi.no/en/statistics-and-analysis/statistics/
(8) Abebe DS. Public Health Challenges of Immigrants in Norway: A Research Review. The Norwegian Centre for Minority Health Research (NAKMI) report 2/2010. Available from: http://www.nakmi.no/publikasjoner/dokumenter/Public-Health-Challenges-of-Immigrants-in-Norway-nakmireport-2-2010.pdf
(9) Kumar BN, Grotvedt L, Meyer HE, Sogaard AJ, Strand BH. The Oslo immigrant health profile. Norwegian Institute of Public Health. Report. 2008: 7. Available from: https://www.fhi.no/globalassets/dokumenterfiler/moba/pdf/rapport-20087-pdf3.pdf
(10) Bloom S 2010
(11) Syse A, Strand BH, Steingrimsdottir OA, Kumar BN. Demographic Research. 2016; 34(22).
(12) Diaz E, Calderón-Larrañaga A, Prado-Torres A, Poblador-Pou B, Gimeno-Feliu LA. How do immigrants use primary healthcare services? A register-based study in Norway. European Journal Public Health: 2014; 25(1): 72-78.
(13) Elstad JI, Finnvold JE, Texmon I. Hogskolen i Oslo og Akerhus. Bruk av sykehus og spesialisthelsetjenester blant innbyggere med norsk og utenlandsk bakgrunn. NOVA Rapport 10/2015. Available from: http://www.hioa.no/Om-HiOA/Senter-for-velferds-og-arbeidslivsforskning/NOVA/Publikasjonar/Rapporter/2015/Bruk-av-sykehus-og-spesialisthelsetjenester-blant-innbyggere-med-norsk-og-utenlandsk-bakgrunn
(14) Norman P, Boyle P, Rees P. Selective migration. Health and deprivation: a longitudinal analysis. Social Science & Medicine. 2004; 2755-2771.
(15) Norredam ML, Neilsen AS, Krasnik A. Migrants' access to healthcare. Danish Medical Bulletin. 2007; 54(1): 48-9.

CHAPTER 10

Health research among migrants in Portugal: insights on current knowledge and future directions

Sónia Dias, Ana Gama, Luis Roxo,
Inês Fronteira, Jorge Simões

Global Health and Tropical Medicine, Instituto de Higiene e Medicina Tropical, Universidade NOVA de Lisboa, Portugal

In an increasingly globalized world, migrants and other mobile individuals are an expanding population of growing social, demographic and political importance, with influence in shaping global health (1,2). In 2015, 4.7 million people migrated to a European Union (EU) member state, including 2.4 million citizens from non-member countries (3). In Portugal, estimates indicate that there were 397,731 legally resident foreign citizens in 2016, most from Brazil, Portuguese-speaking African countries, Eastern Europe, China and a variety of other countries and regions (4).

Increasing evidence has shown that the health of migrants upon arrival in the host country is generally good, and frequently better for certain indicators compared to the general population (5,6). However, research suggests that migrants' health status tends to deteriorate over time after arrival (5,6). Also, some studies point to migrants' vulnerability to poor health considering several indicators (7,8), particularly those related to infectious diseases (9). Indeed, in the host country migrants may face adverse contexts of poor living conditions, economic hardship and social exclusion, that along with separation from family, social networks and lack of social support render these populations more vulnerable to ill health (8). Simultaneously, migrants often experience barriers to accessing health services (10) and the lack of inclusive policies aggravate inequities in health services use (5, 8). In this sense, improving migrants' health and ensuring access to quality health care are essential aspects for integration and social inclusion (11).

Nowadays, human mobility and migratory flows bring relevant challenges to public health in tackling social determinants of health, planning and implementing effective health policies, and adapting the health system to respond to disparate health needs and capacitate health professionals to deal with cultural diversity. Policies that promote effective migrant integration, as well as quality and equity in health care provision are key to attain population's health and well-being. In this context, migrant-sensitive policies must be informed by the produced evidence on health needs, difficulties and barriers to health care faced by migrants in host countries.

In this chapter, we aim to review current knowledge on migrants' health in Portugal and understand future research steps. The chapter is constituted by three sections: 1) a brief overview of migrant health policy in Portugal; 2) national evidence about migrants' health status, access and utilization of health services; and 3) reflections on possible future directions on research susceptible of being translated into evidence-based health policy and practice to reduce health inequalities.

Health policies in Portugal

Over the past years, efforts were made in Portugal to adopt inclusive policies and regulations aiming to promote migrants' access to health services, as expressed in several Constitution articles, decree-laws, dispatch-laws and operational circulars for health services (Figure 1). The Revision of the Portuguese Constitution, in 1989, established that the National Health Service (NHS) is universal and "tendentiously" free of charge, taking into account citizens' social and economic conditions; Portuguese citizens and legal foreign residents are considered equal and have similar civil, social and economic rights (12).

According to Order no. 25360/2001 (16th November 2001) issued by the Ministry of Health, immigrants have the right to access health services and to obtain general health care in a NHS health centre or hospital.

Health services cannot refuse treatment based on nationality, lack of economic means, or undocumented status. Undocumented migrants have full access to NHS once they obtain a health card (or an equivalent document) after proof of over 90 days of residence in Portugal, while those unable to prove it are granted access to health services with full payment. Undocumented migrants may be fee exempt in specific situations, such as in cases of infectious diseases, pregnancy, children under 12 years old, vaccination or victims of human trafficking. Currently, the Portuguese immigration policy is guided by Law No. 29/2012 (9th August 2012) that regulates the conditions and procedures on the entry, stay, exit and removal of foreign citizens from the Portuguese territory. This law establishes that immigrants have access to the health system similarly to Portuguese citizens.

Figure 1. On overview of migrant-friendly policies in Portugal

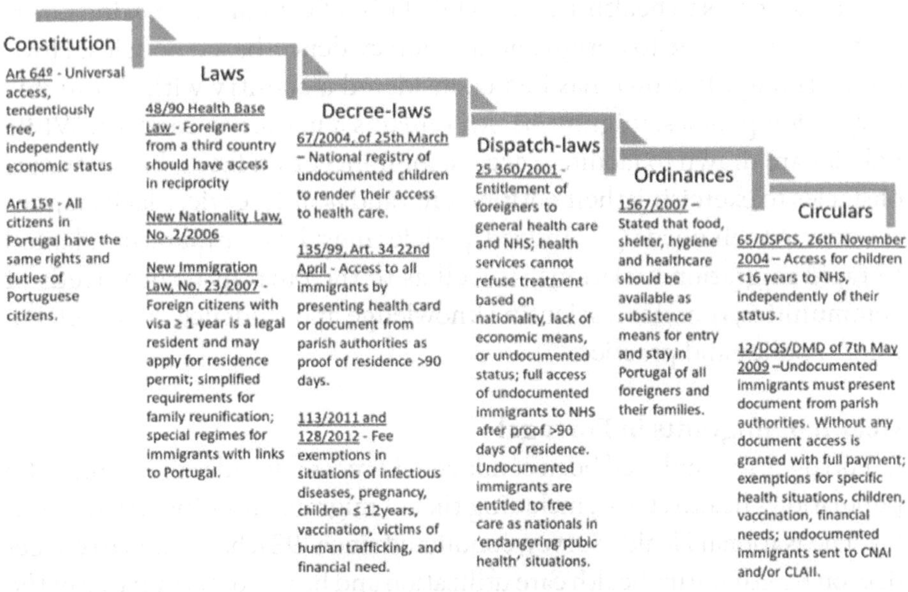

In addition, in 2007 the High Commissariat for Immigration and Intercultural Dialogue (currently named High Commission for Migration) was constituted with the aim of collaborating on the determination, execution

and assessment of policies relevant to the integration of migrants, through regular strategic plans for migration. At the time, this public institution developed a migrant integration plan that comprised labour and professional training, housing, education and health as areas for action. The main goals were to improve immigrants' knowledge of health care services and promote access to migrant-friendly primary health care centres and hospitals. A second plan was developed in 2010 with two additional fields of intervention: promotion of diversity and interculturality, and the healthy ageing of migrants. A third plan was developed in 2015 and aimed to deepen the policy lines regarding management of migratory fluxes and migrant integration.

Overall, Portuguese legislation has acknowledged migrant needs and the role of good health status in their integration (13). Over the years, Portugal has been praised for developing and implementing inclusive policies, protecting migrants' rights, fighting discrimination and promoting migrants' access to health services (13). This reflects the increasing effort that has been made to design and develop evidence-based policies. However, although Portugal has been considered a country with favourable integration policies, migrant health remains a matter of concern. While policies are drawn to facilitate access, migrants often face administrative obstacles to exercising their entitlements and health services lack responsiveness to their needs (14). Indeed, policies must be continuously adapted to rapid migration variations, as well as to the current health needs of communities; therefore, scientific knowledge and evidence are crucial to inform policy and practice.

Health of migrants in Portugal

In Portugal, research had been conducted in recent decades to examine the population's health status, including that of migrants residing in the country. The National Health Survey, conducted since 1987, has aimed to collect data on health status, health care utilization and health determinants of the population residing in Portugal (15). For this chapter, we analysed data from the 5th National Health Survey, carried out in 2014, which included a representative sample of the population in Portugal and a proportion of immigrants (7.3%) close to that in official registries (OCDE). Table 1 presents the sociodemographic characteristics and health indicators of both national and immigrant samples included in the 5th National Health Survey. The immigrant sample obtained was younger than the Portuguese population: while 20.4% of immigrants were aged 15-34, this proportion was lower among nationals (17.7%), and 68.7% of immigrants were 35-64 years old in contrast with 49.4% of nationals in the same age group. There were also more migrants with higher education (28.1%) and higher income (26.4%) than Portuguese respondents (13.5% and 18.0%, respectively).

Results show that immigrants reported better health status than nationals for several indicators (Table 1). While 64.8% of immigrants reported good/very good health status, only 42.9% of nationals reported this. Chronic diseases (diabetes, asthma, hypertension, etc.) were also less frequently reported by immigrants (49.8%) than nationals (62.1%). Regarding mental health, the proportion of participants reporting having felt depressed more than half the days over the previous two weeks was lower among immigrants (5.9%) than among nationals (10.2%). Overall, whether immigrant or Portuguese, health status was reportedly better among persons with higher income and higher educational level (not shown in table), thus highlighting the relevance of these two social determinants of health. Additional analyses of migrant data were performed to understand how their health status evolves over length of time in Portugal. According to the data, 86.6% of immigrants living in Portugal for <6 years reported good/very good health status, while this proportion was lower among immigrants living in the country for >30 years (57.4%). These findings oppose the "popular" idea that migrants arriving are ill or "bring diseases" and burden the health services of the host countries. On the other hand, over time living in Portugal, the percentage of immigrants reporting good/very good health status gets closer to that of the national population (42.9%), as shown in table 1. Similar results were found for chronic diseases and mental health.

As higher length of time living in the host country is linked to increasing age, analyses were replicated with data stratified by age. While the percentage of young (15-34 years old) nationals and migrants reporting good/very good health status was similar (around 82%), migrants aged 35-64 and over 64 reported good health status more frequently (61.7% and 51.4%, respectively) than national counterparts (47.4% and 14.8%, respectively) (data not shown in table).

Table 1. Sociodemographic characteristics, self-reported health status, self-reported chronic disease and self-reported mental health status of national and immigrant respondents, and by immigrants' length of time in Portugal (5th National Health Survey).

					Immigrants' length of time in Portugal (n=1331)							
	Nationals (n=16871)		Immigrants (n=1331)		Less than 6 years (n=67)		6 to 15 years (n=379)		16 to 30 years (n=293)		More than 30 years (n=565)	
	n	%	n	%	n	%	n	%	n	%	n	%
Gender												
Male	7376	43.7	567	42.6	33	49.3	174	45.9	124	42.3	226	40.0
Female	9495	56.3	764	57.4	34	50.7	205	54.1	169	57.7	339	60.0
Age												
15-34	2990	17.7	271	20.4	36	53.7	123	32.5	90	30.7	11	1.9
35-64	8326	49.4	915	68.7	29	43.3	228	60.2	171	58.4	475	84.1
> 64	5555	32.9	145	10.9	2	3.0	28	7.4	32	10.9	79	14.0
Educational level												
No educational level	2323	13.8	26	2.0	1	1.5	3	0.8	4	1.4	17	3.0
1st grade – 6th grade	7026	41.6	208	15.6	13	19.4	51	13.5	40	13.7	98	17.3
7th grade – 9th grade	2783	16.5	294	22.1	16	23.9	96	25.3	57	19.5	120	21.2
10th grade – 12th grade	2465	14.6	429	32.2	21	31.3	142	37.5	112	38.2	147	26.0
Higher education	2274	13.5	374	28.1	16	23.9	87	23.0	80	27.3	183	32.4
Income												
First quintile (lower income)	3792	22.5	233	17.5	16	23.9	84	22.2	51	17.4	77	13.6
Second quintile	3532	20.9	225	16.9	12	17.9	86	22.7	57	19.5	65	11.5
Third quintile	3326	19.7	270	20.3	17	25.4	78	20.6	62	21.2	109	19.3
Forth quintile	3184	18.9	252	18.9	12	17.9	78	20.6	53	18.1	102	18.1
Fifth quintile (higher income)	3037	18.0	351	26.4	10	14.9	53	14.0	70	23.9	212	37.5
Self-reported health status												
Good/ Very good	7228	42.9	862	64.8	58	86.6	260	68.6	203	69.3	324	57.4
Fair	6727	39.9	380	28.6	8	11.9	97	25.6	76	25.9	191	33.9
Poor/ Very poor	2909	17.2	88	6.6	1	1.5	22	5.8	14	4.8	49	8.7
Chronic disease/ long-term health problem												
Yes	10471	62.1	663	49.8	25	37.3	175	46.2	132	45.1	317	56.1
No	6385	37.9	668	50.2	42	62.7	204	53.8	161	54.9	248	43.9
How often felt depressed last 2 weeks												
Never	10869	64.6	983	74.1	56	83.6	303	80.1	215	73.4	389	69.1
Several days	4227	25.1	265	20.0	9	13.4	63	16.7	61	20.8	127	22.6
More than half the days	1721	10.2	78	5.9	2	3.0	12	3.2	17	5.8	47	8.3

The health outcomes described may be related to the socioeconomic profile of the migrants included in the National Health Survey. Indeed, the sampling frame used in the National Health Survey was based on a sample of households, therefore the survey enrolled migrant populations in a well-established socioeconomic position, with higher level of education, representing a socially advantaged group compared to nationals.

In contrast, other research initiatives have sought to understand health and illness in groups of migrants in a more social disadvantage context. Indeed, several cross-sectional studies using community-based samples or health and social services users' samples have reached groups of migrants in a lower socioeconomic condition, more excluded and vulnerable.

One of those studies was conducted in the region with highest representation and concentration of immigrants in the country (Lisbon and Tagus Valley region) and aimed to obtain information about the health status of a diversified sample of immigrants (16). Data were collected in areas where most immigrants reside, using a snowball sampling procedure in a community-based setting. Overall, 1375 African, Brazilian and Eastern European migrants participated in this study, of whom 35.4% had elementary education, more than a half reported insufficient income, 25.7% were undocumented and about a third were non employed (16). The results showed that, although 61.5% of participants reported good health status, male and female migrants with higher education were more likely to report good health, as well as women with higher income. Other studies in Portugal have also found an association between socioeconomic status and good health for other health indicators, such as hypertension (17), overweight and obesity (18,19), and mental health (20). Research also showed that the prevalence of overweight was lower for migrants than natives, and length of residence was associated with overweight among adult immigrants (21).

Migrating to another country may be a complex and stressful phenomenon due to factors related to the migratory experience, the process of acculturation to the host country and the risk of social exclusion (8,22,23). Indeed, evidence has shown that the experience of migrating may be associated with a higher risk of poor mental health including psychological distress, depressive disorders, bipolar disorder and post-traumatic stress disorder (24–26,22). This risk may continue for second and third generation migrants (26).

In a study conducted to assess psychological stress among African, Brazilian and Eastern European migrants (23), participants were asked how frequent they felt tired, psychologically tired, happy, full of energy or lonely since arriving in Portugal. Overall, 27.9% of the sample reported symptoms of psychological distress. Higher levels of psychological distress were reported by female immigrants, those who were unemployed, socially isolated, with lower income and high job insecurity (23).

Sexual and reproductive health are also a main concern in public health given that it affects directly and indirectly the health and well-being of individuals and communities, and considering that many migrants are of reproductive age (27). A study to assess differences in obstetric care between immigrant and native women showed that immigrant women were more prone to obtain late prenatal care and have intrapartum complications than nationals (28). These findings are in line with a literature review and other studies in Portugal indicating poorer maternal health and higher health risk profile among immigrants (29,30).

Another relevant topic concerning migrants' sexual health relates to HIV infection. Indeed, migrants, particularly those originating from countries with high prevalence of HIV, have been considered one of the key populations more vulnerable to HIV (31). A recent study on HIV, conducted with a venue-based sample of Sub-Saharan African immigrants in great Lisbon, found that HIV infection was 8 times more likely among immigrants with no educational level than among those with secondary/higher education, and was 5 times more likely among those with insufficient income compared to those with sufficient income (32).

Migrants' access to and utilization of health services

Research has also focused on understanding migrants' use of health care services, as access to and utilization of health services are crucial for attaining a good health status.

A retrospective-period prevalence study compared access to preventive health services between migrants and nationals in five EU countries including Portugal, using information from the National Health Survey (33). Portuguese data showed that migrants tend to use health services less frequently than nationals, in particular the preventive care services. Migrants aged 50-74 reported less frequently having performed colorectal cancer screening in the previous 2 years than same-age nationals, and there were also less migrant women (aged 50-69 years old) having performed a mammography over the previous 2 years than national counterparts. The proportion of women aged 20-69 years old who had undertaken a Pap smear test in the previous 3 years was lower among EU-migrant women (50.6%), compared to national (63.2%) and non-EU migrants (63.8%) (33). In the field of maternal and child health, the lower use of health services by migrants compared to nationals has also been described (30).

In a study conducted on patterns of health care use in a community-based sample of migrants, male and recently arrived migrants were more likely to have never used the NHS (34). The gender variation observed in the patterns of health services use is in line with previous studies showing that men (either migrants or nationals) underuse health services when compared with women, who are more likely to report frequent contact with the health system (35,36,10). Other research reporting non-use of health services among those recently arrived has highlighted that this is partially related to lack of knowledge of migrants' health rights and how the health care system functions (37). Less utilization of the NHS among recent immigrants may also be attributable to the 'healthy immigrant effect', according to which these immigrants have better health status than those who have resided in the host country for a longer period (38–40). In fact, these migrants may not need to seek health care because they are healthier and do not consider preventive care a priority while adapting to a new context with other concerns ahead such as housing, employment and social protection (41).

Access to primary health care is fundamental in terms of preventive medicine and an important health equity indicator. Primary health care should be the privileged gateway to health care, providing opportunities for health promotion, disease prevention and early detection of disease (42). In Portugal, an effort has been made in the past decade to strengthen primary health care and improve its accessibility, proximity, quality and equity of care (42,43). However, in the abovementioned study on patterns of health care use, although most participants used primary health care services the first time health care was needed, about one third of the sample reported having used the hospital, mainly male and undocumented migrants (34).

Indeed, migration status has been pointed out as a key factor of migrants' access to health care, being reported that undocumented immigrants are more likely to have never used the NHS and face difficulties in accessing health care services (34). Other studies focused on understanding obstacles in access to health services show that undocumented immigrants are frequently unaware of their health rights, report lack of knowledge on the health services available, and often fear potential implications of being undocumented, such as services' denunciation to authorities and deportation (11,10,44,45).

Other migrant subgroups accumulate health vulnerabilities and risks, which is the case of migrant sex workers, yet they have been understudied (46,47). In a bio-behavioural study on sexual health needs, of migrant sex workers those undocumented reported more frequently having never used health services and having never been tested for HIV, leading to unawareness of their HIV status (48). In fact, among participants with a reactive result to the HIV rapid test, all HIV-positive undocumented migrants were unaware of their seropositivity, and most migrants had never been tested for HIV (48). This result contrasts with the fact that access to HIV rapid test is legally free of charge and confidential in Portugal. The findings suggest that these migrants still face barriers that limit access to HIV testing, such as the 'triple stigma' associated with being undocumented, disclosure of sex-work activity and a possible HIV-positive result, which may turn them reluctant to test for HIV (48–50). In this context, innovative outreach prevention initiatives would be valuable to help access more vulnerable migrant subgroups frequently out of reach of formal health care services.

In order to gain a deeper understanding of migrants' patterns of health services use and barriers to access, qualitative studies have been conducted to explore migrants' perceptions and experiences about health services (51,52). In these studies, positive experiences, especially during pregnancy, were described by immigrants regarding the social support provided and the existence of an appointed family doctor. The degree of satisfaction with health services was found to be strongly influenced by cultural background, expectations and previous experiences in the country of origin. In addition, barriers to access mainly related to unawareness and misinformation among office workers and health professionals about migrants' health rights, and also to structural and functioning characteristics of the services (such as cost, restricted working hours, highly bureaucratic procedures and long waiting time). Actually, most of these constraints are commonly experienced by Portuguese citizens, however they tend to affect migrants differently as these populations often have less labour protection and less flexible work schedules (51).

The perspectives of health professionals on factors influencing migrants' access to and use of health services can also provide insights. A cross-sectional study carried out with a representative sample of 320 health workers from primary health care services in the Lisbon region, including office workers, nurses and doctors, showed that generally most participants considered their knowledge and competencies to deal with migrants to be insufficient and that having specific training on migrants' health would be relevant (53).

How to move forward to reduce health inequalities and promote equity?

Developing meaningful research on migrants' health has several conceptual, methodological and practical challenges (54–57). Besides a common cross-national conceptual framework is still missing, most health data regularly collected at national and EU levels do not include variables related to migration, thus hindering stratification of health data by migration features. Indeed, some challenges in several studies is the low representation of migrants, including those more vulnerable, such as undocumented and newly arrived, migrants.

In addition, population-based statistics commonly use 'citizenship' and in this context, for example, ethnic groups are difficult to classify. Also, in terms of instruments used to collect data, surveys lack international standardized approaches for monitoring variables and indicators related to health of migrants and validated questionnaires for cross-cultural use. A complex and diverse set of definitions, terms, categories and labels (e.g. 'immigrants', 'migrants', 'foreign born', 'foreign origin', 'second generation', 'ethnic minority', among others) are used across countries. Migrants' differing conceptions of health are difficult to evaluate. Moreover, a difficulty remains in recruiting undocumented, newly arrived and other difficult-to-access migrant subgroups. Lack of communities' involvement, as well as linguistic and cultural issues, are still barriers to enrol migrants. Privacy and confidentiality are also major concerns in health research with migrant populations. In addition, practical challenges include the logistical and financial difficulties of creating and maintaining comprehensive databases.

Notwithstanding, the current knowledge reinforces that although migrants, and particularly those newly arrived, report in general good health status, health inequities persist and some groups remain more vulnerable (10,16,34). Frequently, it is manifest that practice does not reflect policy, which may mean that knowledge produced may not be sufficient to design effective interventions and reduce the policy-practice gap.

In fact, there is still great difficulty in answering key questions such as: 'How to tackle migrants' heterogeneity?'; 'How to research most vulnerable, understudied and underserved subgroups?'; 'How to further understand the contexts that increase vulnerability?'; 'How to overcome health inequalities?'; 'How to put the results into practice and translate them into effective interventions? '; and 'What needs to be done differently to achieve true equity and effective health gains?'.

Blind spots where more research and comprehensive data is needed have been identified and include background information, especially regarding migration variables such as type of migrant, reasons for migration, migration history, and integration into host country (55–57). Further research should also focus on examining different patterns of health and illness over time (56). Furthermore, exploring the impact of migration on epidemiological situation and health outcomes in origin and host countries (through remittances, technology transfer and behaviour change) is needed (56,57). In this sense, a greater diversity on study design is required, namely longitudinal and mixed-method studies, capable of providing a deeper insight on the needs of migrants. Research projects about migration and health must also take into account other approaches, namely evaluation research, life course approach, translational research with origin, transit and host countries, and the inclusion of migrants in epidemiological monitoring systems.

In face of the lack of adequate data available that could provide an accurate and useful picture of communities' health needs, it has been emphasized the importance of improving data and knowledge base, and mechanisms for measuring, monitoring, evaluating and reporting data on migrants' health (55–57). This calls for new ways to develop information base and surveillance of migrants' health.

Part of the challenge is in shifting the research paradigm and invest in innovative forms of producing useful and relevant knowledge. It has been increasingly advocated the need of involving all stakeholders (communities, policy makers, researchers and health professionals) to produce knowledge that is translatable into evidence-based policies and intervention models that effectively respond to communities' needs, contribute to improve their health and promote social change. In this context, most recent research has been developed with a participatory approach. Experience has shown the participatory approach to be a good way for promoting equity, since it is based on the principle that partnership is established with all stakeholders and all participate equitably (58–60).

Involving communities (including migrants, community-based organizations, health professionals, policy makers and academics), for example, in the construction of data collection instruments and in the discussion about the best approach to reach a diverse sample of participants and increase their adhesion, including those most at risk, may allow to design more culturally adapted research projects and obtain more reliable and relevant data (59,61). Additionally, this process leads to increased partners' ownership of and involvement in the project (61,62). This contributes to communities' empowerment and capacity building for advocating for their health rights and health promotion, and the knowledge created becomes potentially more useful as it meets the real needs of communities (59,61).

The translation of the produced knowledge into policies, services and in the communities can also be discussed through a participatory approach. Notwithstanding, assessment of the results and impact of projects is crucial to expand the use of participatory research and maximize its potential for informing effective actions that improve health (58,59).

Globally, rethinking directions in research to inform policies and effective practices is needed, which includes: developing EU cross-national surveys related to health and social issues, given the need for a common framework for comparative research on international health, migration and ethnic diversity; measuring health outcomes and related factors, their mechanisms and trends over time; building partnerships and active collaboration with communities to design and implement research that addresses relevant research questions, using efficient and culturally adapted methodologies to reach most vulnerable, understudied and underserved subgroups; promoting knowledge translation; conducting implementation research to understand what, why, and how policies, programs and interventions work in "real world" settings and test approaches to improve them; and developing evaluation research for critical assessment of policy frameworks, 'good practices' and responses of host health systems to manage the needs of migrants.

The increasing and complex dynamics of migratory flows, as well as its links to population health vulnerabilities reinforce the continuing need for development of data collection, monitoring and surveillance mechanisms to better understand populations' health needs and inform effective health policies and practices. Ultimately, reducing health inequities and improving health care among vulnerable groups, including migrants, is key to obtain health gains for the whole population.

Acknowledgements??

References

(1) Gushulak BD, MacPherson DW. The basic principles of migration health: Population mobility and gaps in disease prevalence. Emerg Themes Epidemiol. 2006;3(3).

(2) MacPherson DW, Gushulak BD, Macdonald L. Health and foreign policy: Influences of migration and population mobility. Bull World Health Organ. 2007;85:200–6.

(3) Eurostat. Migration and migrant population statistics. 2017 [Accessed 2018 Jan 22]. Available from: http://ec.europa.eu/eurostat/statistics-explained/index.php/Migration_and_migrant_population_statistics

(4) SEF/GEPF. Relatório de Imigração, Fronteiras e Asilo - 2016. Lisbon: SEF. 2017 p. 1-84. Available from: http://sefstat.sef.pt/Docs/Rifa2016.pdf

(5) Giannoni M, Franzini L, Masiero G. Migrant integration policies and health inequalities in Europe. BMC Public Health. 2016;16(1):463.

(6) Marceca M. Migration and Health from a Public Health Perspective. In: Muenstermann I, editor. People's Movements in the 21st Century - Risks, Challenges and Benefits. InTech; 2017.

(7) Nielsen SS, Krasnik A. Poorer self-perceived health among migrants and ethnic minorities versus the majority population in Europe: a systematic review. Int J Public Health. 2010;55(5):357–71.
(8) Rechel B, Mladovsky P, Ingleby D, Mackenbach JP, McKee M. Migration and health in an increasingly diverse Europe. Lancet. 2013 Apr;381(9873):1235–45.
(9) Desgrées-du-Loû A, Pannetier J, Ravalihasy A, Gosselin A, Supervie V, Panjo H, et al. Sub-Saharan African migrants living with HIV acquired after migration, France, ANRS PARCOURS study, 2012 to 2013. Eurosurveillance. 2015;20(46):30065.
(10) Dias SF, Severo M, Barros H. Determinants of health care utilization by immigrants in Portugal. BMC Health Serv Res. 2008 Dec 7;8:207.
(11) Ingleby D, Chimienti M, Hatziprokopiou P, Ormond M, de Freitas C. The role of health in integration. In: Fonseca ML, Malheiros J, editors. Social integration and mobility: education, housing and health IMISCOE Cluster B5 State of the art report. Lisbon: Centro de Estudos Geográficos; 2005. p. 101–37.
(12) Simoes J de A, Figueiredo Augusto G, Fronteira I, Hernandez-Quevedo C. Portugal: Health System Review. Health Syst Transit. 2017 Mar;19(2):1–184.
(13) World Health Organization Regional Office for Europe. Portugal: assessing health-system capacity to manage sudden large influxes of migrants. Copenhagen: World Health Organization. 2014 p. 1-10. Available from: http://www.euro.who.int/__data/assets/pdf_file/0016/265012/Portugal-assessing-health-system-capacity-to-manage-sudden-large-influxes-of-migrants.pdf
(14) Migration Policy Group. Migrant Integration Policy Index (MIPEX) 2015 - Portugal [Accessed 2018 Jan 22]. Available from: http://www.mipex.eu/portugal
(15) Dias CM. 25 anos de Inquérito Nacional de Saúde em Portugal. Rev Port Saúde Pública. 2009;51–60.
(16) Dias S, Gama A, Martins MO. Health status and preventative behaviors of immigrants by gender and origin: A Portuguese cross-sectional study. Nurs Health Sci. 2013 Sep;15(3):309–17.
(17) Peixoto C, Carrilho G, Alarcão V, Guerra F, Simões R, Fernandes M, et al. PRAdA Intervention: Effects on weight of dietary intervention among treated hypertensive Portuguese natives and African immigrants. Acta Med Port. 2014;27(3):331–41.
(18) Goulão B, Santos O, Alarcão V, Portugal R, Carreira M, do Carmo I. Prevalência de excesso de peso nos imigrantes brasileiros e africanos residentes em Portugal. Rev Port Saúde Pública. 2015 Jan;33(1):24–32.
(19) Lopes E, Alarcão V, Simões R, Fernandes M, Gómez V, Souto D, et al. Controlo da Hipertensão Arterial nos Cuidados de Saúde Primários: Uma

Comparação entre Nativos Portugueses e Imigrantes dos Países Africanos de Língua Oficial Portuguesa. Acta Med Port. 2016 Mar 31;29(3):193–204.

(20) Pussetti C. Identidades em Crise: imigrantes, emoções e saúde mental em Portugal. Saúde e Soc. 2010;19(1):94–113.

(21) da Costa LP, Dias SF, Martins M do RO. Association between length of residence and overweight among adult immigrants in Portugal: A nationwide cross-sectional study. BMC Public Health. 2017 Dec 13;17(1):316.

(22) Lindert J, Schouler-Ocak M, Heinz A, Priebe S. Mental health, health care utilisation of migrants in Europe. Eur Psychiatry. 2008 Jan;23(Supp 1): 14–20.

(23) Teixeira AF, Dias SF. Labor market integration, immigration experience, and psychological distress in a multi-ethnic sample of immigrants residing in Portugal. Ethn Health. 2016 Jan 2;23(1):81–96.

(24) Bustamante LHU, Cerqueira RO, Leclerc E, Brietzke E. Stress, trauma, and posttraumatic stress disorder in migrants: a comprehensive review. Rev Bras Psiquiatr. 2017 Oct 19;Epub.

(25) Dalgard OS, Thapa S. Immigration, social integration and mental health in Norway, with focus on gender differences. Clin Pract Epidemiol Ment Heal. 2007;3:24.

(26) Guardia D, Salleron J, Roelandt J-L, Vaiva G. [Prevalence of psychiatric and substance use disorders among three generations of migrants: Results from French population cohort]. Encephale. 2016 Oct;43(5):435–43.

(27) UNFPA - United Nations Population Fund. State of World Population 2006 - A Passage to Hope: Women and International Migration. New York: UNFPA. 2006 p 1-107. Available from: http://www.unfpa.org/sites/default/files/pub-pdf/sowp06-en.pdf

(28) Almeida LM, Santos CC, Caldas JP, Ayres-de-Campos D, Dias S. Obstetric care in a migrant population with free access to health care. Int J Gynecol Obstet. 2014 Sep;126(3):244–7.

(29) Almeida LM, Caldas J, Ayres-de-Campos D, Salcedo-Barrientos D, Dias S. Maternal Healthcare in Migrants: A Systematic Review. Matern Child Health J. 2013 Oct 20;17(8):1346–54.

(30) Machado M do C, Santana P, Carreiro MH, Nogueira H, Barroso MR, Dias A. Iguais ou diferentes? Cuidados de saúde materno-infantil a uma população de imigrantes. Lisbon: Bial; 2006.

(31) European Centre for Disease Prevention and Control/ WHO Regional Office for Europe. HIV/AIDS surveillance in Europe 2015. Solna: European Centre for Disease Prevention and Control. 2016 p. 1-195. Available from: http://ecdc.europa.eu/en/publications/Publications/HIV-AIDS-surveillance-Europe-2015.pdf

(32) Dias S. Migrantes Africanos e Infeção VIH: estudo de prevalência e factores associados. In: 4o Congresso Nacional de Medicina Tropical. Lisbon, Portugal; 2017.
(33) Rosano A, Dauvrin M, Buttigieg SC, Ronda E, Tafforeau J, Dias S. Migrant's access to preventive health services in five EU countries. BMC Health Serv Res. 2017 Dec 23;17:588.
(34) Dias S, Gama A, Cortes M, de Sousa B. Healthcare-seeking patterns among immigrants in Portugal. Heal Soc Care Community. 2011;19(5):514–21.
(35) DuBard CA, Massing MW. Trends in emergency Medicaid expenditures for recent and undocumented immigrants. JAMA. 2007 Mar 14;297(10):1085.
(36) Fenta H, Hyman I, Noh S. Health service utilization by Ethiopian immigrants and refugees in Toronto. J Immigr Minor Heal. 2007 Aug 7;9(4):349–57.
(37) Cots F, Castells X, García O, Riu M, Felipe A, Vall O. Impact of immigration on the cost of emergency visits in Barcelona (Spain). BMC Health Serv Res. 2007 Dec 19;7:9.
(38) Sundquist J. Migration, equality and access to health care services. J Epidemiol Community Heal. 2001 Oct 1;(10):691–2.
(39) Muennig P, Fahs MC. Health status and hospital utilization of recent immigrants to New York City. Prev Med. 2002 Sep;35(3):225–31.
(40) Lucas JW, Barr-Anderson DJ, Kington RS. Health status, health insurance, and health care utilization patterns of immigrant black men. Am J Public Health. 2003 Oct;93(10):1740–7.
(41) Diaz E, Kumar BN. Differential utilization of primary health care services among older immigrants and Norwegians: a register-based comparative study in Norway. BMC Health Serv Res. 2014 Dec 26;14(1):623.
(42) World Health Organization. The world health report 2008 - primary health care (now more than ever). Geneva: World Health Organization. 2008. Available from: http://www.who.int/whr/2008/en/
(43) Ministério da Saúde. Reforma do Serviço Nacional de Saúde - Coordenação nacional para os Cuidados de Saúde Primários. Plano Estratégico e Operacional. Lisbon: Ministério da Saúde; 2016 p. 1-6. Available from: https://www.sns.gov.pt/wp-content/uploads/2016/02/Plano_Estrategico_e_Operacional.pdf
(44) Manfellotto D. Case study 5: From misinformation and ignorance to recognition and care: Immigrants and homeless in Rome, Italy in health systems confront poverty. In: Barbosa R, Charpak Y, Turner S, Ziglio E, editors. Poverty and health: Evidence and action in WHO's European region. Copenhagen: World Health Organization Regional Office for Europe; 2002. p. 49–56.
(45) Gonçalves A, Dias S, Luck M, Fernandes MJ, Cabral J. Acesso aos cuidados de saúde de comunidades migrantes: problemas e perspectivas de intervenção. Rev Port Saúde Pública. 2003;21(1):55–64.

(46) Platt L, Grenfell P, Bonell C, Creighton S, Wellings K, Parry J, et al. Risk of sexually transmitted infections and violence among indoor-working female sex workers in London: the effect of migration from Eastern Europe. Sex Transm Infect. 2011 Aug 1;87(5):377–84.

(47) Richter M, Chersich MF, Vearey J, Sartorius B, Temmerman M, Luchters S. Migration status, work conditions and health utilization of female sex workers in three South African cities. J Immigr Minor Heal. 2014 Feb 13;16:7–17.

(48) Dias S, Gama A, Pingarilho M, Simões D, Mendão L. Health services use and HIV prevalence among migrant and national female sex workers in Portugal: Are we providing the services needed? AIDS Behav. 2017 Aug 30;21(8):2316–21.

(49) Blondell SJ, Kitter B, Griffin MP, Durham J. Barriers and facilitators to HIV testing in migrants in high-income countries: A systematic review. AIDS Behav. 2015 Nov 30;19(11):2012–24.

(50) Wang Y, Li B, Zheng J, Sengupta S, Emrick CB, Cohen MS, et al. Factors related to female sex workers' willingness to utilize VCT service: A qualitative study in Jinan City, Northern China. AIDS Behav. 2009 Oct 4;13(5):866–72.

(51) Dias S, Gama A, Rocha C. Immigrant women's perceptions and experiences of health care services: Insights from a focus group study. J Public Health. 2010 Oct 21;18(5):489–96.

(52) Almeida LM, Casanova C, Caldas J, Ayres-de-Campos D, Dias S. Migrant women's perceptions of healthcare during pregnancy and early motherhood: Addressing the social determinants of health. J Immigr Minor Heal. 2014 Aug 25;16(4):719–23.

(53) Dias S, Gama A, Cargaleiro H, Martins MO. Health workers' attitudes toward immigrant patients: a cross-sectional survey in primary health care services. Hum Resour Health. 2012 Dec 9;10(1):14.

(54) Abebe DS. Public health challenges of immigrants in Norway: A research review. Oslo: NAKMI. 2010 p. 1-79. Available from: https://www.nakmi.no/publikasjoner/dokumenter/Public-Health-Challenges-of-Immigrants-in-Norway-nakmireport-2-2010.pdf

(55) Ingleby D. European Research on Migration and Health – Background Paper. Brussels: International Organization for Migration. 2009 p. 1-30. Available from: http://www.migrant-health-europe.org/files/Research on Migrant Health_Background Paper.pdf

(56) Juhász J, Makara P, Taller Á. Possibilities and limitations of comparative research on international migration and health [Working paper]. PROMINSTAT. 2010. Available from: https://ec.europa.eu/migrant-integration/index.cfm?action=media.download&uuid=2A1598BB-9B89-885E-D1EBE09AEB3F086F

(57) Tulloch O, Machingura F, Melamed C. Health, migration and the 2030 Agenda for Sustainable Development. London: Overseas Development Institute. 2016 p. 1-13. Available from: https://www.odi.org/sites/odi.org.uk/files/resource-documents/10759.pdf
(58) Cargo M, Mercer SL. The value and challenges of participatory research: Strengthening its practice. Annu Rev Public Health. 2008 Apr;29(1):325–50.
(59) Dias S, Gama A. [Community-based participatory research in public health: potentials and challenges]. Rev Panam Salud Pública. 2014;35(2):150–4.
(60) Wallerstein NB, Duran B. Using community-based participatory research to address health disparities. Health Promot Pract. 2006 Jul 30;7(3):312–23.
(61) Strauss RP, Sengupta S, Quinn SC, Goeppinger J, Spaulding C, Kegeles SM, et al. The role of community advisory boards: Involving communities in the informed consent process. Am J Public Health. 2001 Dec;91(12):1938–43.
(62) Parrado EA, McQuiston C, Flippen CA. Participatory survey research: Integrating community collaboration and quantitative methods for the study of gender and HIV risks among Hispanic migrants. Sociol Methods Res. 2005 Nov 30;34(2):204–39.